First published in the UK in 2004 by Circle Books
Circle Books
83/84 George Street
Richmond
Surrey TW9 1HE
Phone: 020 8332 2709

© British Sub-Aqua Club
Telford's Quay, South Pier Road
Ellesmere Port
Cheshire CH65 4FL
Phone: 0151 350 6200

Author
Deric Ellerby

Editor
Paul Critcher

Art Editor
Alistair Cook

Illustrations: Ian Legge
Source illustrations: Daphne Ellerby

Print
Printed in China for Compass Press Limited
100-104 Upper Richmond Road
London SW15 2SP
Phone: 020 8780 7000

ISBN: 0-9538919-4-1

Dive leading

Advance your diving skills

Foreword

Once divers have acquired the basic knowledge and skills to dive safely, it is natural that they should want to broaden their experience of the underwater world. This manual has been written for such divers, to assist them to gain the necessary additional knowledge and skills. In doing so their increased experience will not only provide a greater awareness of the underwater environment, but also equip them to lead others to share their experience. Extending skills and awareness of the diversity of diving available to recreational divers should always be done as safely as possible, utilising the knowledge and experience of instructors or other more experienced divers. This manual contains a wealth of advice and guidance for divers keen to progress further. I hope it will inspire you to go out and do the real thing – diving!

National Diving Officer Lizzie Bird

Table of contents

Table of contents

Table of contents

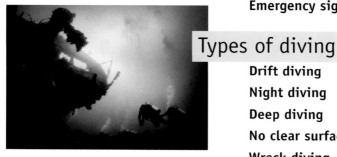

Introduction
What is a dive leader?

What is a dive leader?

To be able to make controlling decisions about the conduct of a dive demands certain levels of knowledge, skill and experience. Attaining this level is not something that occurs at one particular moment, with the mastery of a certain skill, the passing of an assessment or the logging of a particular number of dives. It is a gradual process of increasing ability, of taking on more personal responsibility until you reach a level where you can safely lead yourself and a suitably qualified buddy on a particular dive. The dive will need to be one that is well within your experience and in an underwater environment with which you are already familiar. Your buddy will need to be at least at a similar diving experience level as you, but it is the moment you have been waiting for.

Knowledge

So what are these levels of knowledge, skill and experience? First of all let's establish how advanced your diving is. Divers who have covered all the topics in the first book in this series, *The Diving Manual*, should certainly have attained enough skills and knowledge to start on the dive-leading ladder. Regardless of whether you've read the book or not, you should be proficient in basic underwater skills such as good buoyancy control, be familiar with equipment, and have an understanding of the effects of nitrogen, pressure and the causes of decompression sickness. You should also be aware of the environment in which you are diving and the safety procedures, such as buddy diving, that divers employ.

If you've reached this level of competence in your diving, then you are ready to move on to dive leading. To safely control a dive means having the theoretical knowledge required to plan the dive. You will need to be able to calculate the breathing-gas requirements for the desired depth and time and to calculate the decompression requirements of the dive. You will also need to be able to anticipate the effects of weather and tide on both the surface and underwater conditions at the chosen site. A prior knowledge of the area will enable you to confidently navigate underwater and safely cope with water access and exit, as well as being confident it is within the capabilities of yourself and your buddy.

Typically, this personal development will not be happening in isolation. You should be diving with either the close support of a diving club or a diving school. Making best use of instructors and experienced divers will greatly assist you in gaining the necessary knowledge and skills, as well as providing you with an objective assessment of your progress. An essential aspect of your development will be gaining experience at as wide a variety of diving sites as possible. It is also important to undertake dives with a variety of different purposes to broaden your range of skills. You should take every opportunity to understand, and if possible experience, a broad range of diving equipment. □

A wealth of new experiences awaits the dive leader

Chapter one
Planning
the dive

One of the most important
aspects of diving is the
planning, and divers should
pay close attention to it.
A variety of factors needs
to be taken into account
when preparing for dives.
Where will we enter and
exit the water? How will
we get there? How will we
locate our specific dive site?
These are just some of the
questions which will need
to be answered before
you have even put your
equipment on. You will find
that good preparation will
lead to the best diving in
safe conditions.

Planning the dive
Dive planning

Divers receive a briefing

Dive planning falls into two main areas, planning for the group and planning for individual buddy pairs.

Planning for a group of divers demands consideration of a range of factors. The experience and capability of each diver must first be considered. This is then used to check and confirm or otherwise the suitability of the site for each diver, or the diver for the planned site. This same assessment of each diver's strengths and weaknesses is then used to ensure that appropriate buddy pairings are made. While each individual diver must have the necessary skills and experience needed to safely participate in the dive, it is also important that the buddy pair has the capability to support one another in acting autonomously. Even on dives in calm waters with excellent visibility, with groups of divers led by a guide, there is benefit from

buddy pairing within the group. While the dive guide or instructor will be keeping an overall watch on the group, two paired divers can more easily keep an eye on one another and offer immediate assistance, even if that is alerting the dive guide to a possible problem.

In situations where diver separation is more likely, such as in lower visibility or when diving in moving water, then buddy pairs are the most sensible grouping. Keeping an eye on just one other diver is much simpler and makes for a much more enjoyable dive and a more certain level of buddy support. When planning dives for groups of divers there must always be enough experienced divers to cope with the needs of those with lesser experience. The person in overall charge of the diving operation will need sufficient experience and knowledge of the individuals making

Your choice of dive site will have a direct bearing on how you access it, be it a sandy beach (left) or a rocky shoreline (right), especially in shore-based diving

up the group in order to make decisions on buddy pairings and the final composition of the group. This supervisor is often referred to as the dive marshal, and in deciding on dive pairings for particular sites, he or she will need to have a detailed knowledge of the site. Depth ranges, underwater visibility and water movement will be important factors influencing which groups and individuals should dive a site under the prevailing conditions. Similarly, the existing and forecast weather conditions may also have a strong bearing on such decisions. While it is good and necessary that divers extend their previous diving range and practice, this must always be done in a gradual, progressive manner. Being paired with a diver who has already successfully participated in diving the particular site is an obvious way of gaining new experience.

Site choice and access

These two items are often interdependent, the possibility of diving a specific site being conditional upon access to it by your diving team. It is useful to consider two main categories of site in this context,

shore-based diving and boat-based diving.

Shore-based diving is usually the simpler and least expensive option, unless you are choosing somewhere pretty adventurous and exotic. It is often possible to transport both equipment and divers directly to an entry point without needing to use anything other than normal vehicles. While divers aim to be weightless in the water, our equipment is both bulky and weighty, so minimising carrying distance on land is highly desirable. The next important factors in the choice of a shore-based site are the entry and exit points. While it is possible to jump into the water from moderate heights, as a fully equipped diver the reverse is not true. So, before any entry is made it is essential that there is a convenient point to exit the water close at hand – just in case of problems.

Besides access and exit, a major factor in choosing the dive site will be its interest to the diver. As a place to practise skills the site should have calm water, reasonable visibility, suitable depth, temperature and a convenient distance from home. Or it could be the attraction of the marine life in that spot, a shipwreck or other personal-interest reasons. As a place to develop your diving it may well be chosen to offer different

Site fixing

In tidal waters it is important to be able to predict tidal conditions

experience from previously used sites. Changed diving conditions may also demand changes to equipment, such as moving from a wetsuit to a drysuit or vice versa, use of a distance line in low visibility, or a surface marker buoy. If these are new experiences then additional training will be needed.

For most sites it is easy to find someone who has previous knowledge of the area and can advise on the diving conditions likely to be met. In tidal waters it is very important to know what currents are expected, in order to be able to predict tidal slack water and understand the likely effect of particular wave action, both underwater and on the surface. Where local knowledge is not available – and sometimes even when it is – it is useful to be able to use a chart and to understand the basic topography of the area. This will help in predicting the likely nature of the dive site besides giving you clues as to the type of underwater conditions you can expect.

A conventional surface swimmer can manage a speed of around 1m (metre) per second but will find this fairly tiring over extended periods. Add full diving equipment and even using fins the same person will find even half that speed difficult to maintain for any extended period of time. Converting this into nautical measurements we can see that most divers can manage to swim underwater against a 0.5-knot current and experienced divers may even cope with 1 knot for a short time, though not without a fair amount of stress and some judicious handholds. Anything faster than 1 knot is likely to be very hard work and possible only for a very limited time. Given this performance it is easy to see why we need some knowledge of the strength and direction of water currents at a dive site.

Site fixing

Maritime charts are devised to aid shipping rather than divers, but nonetheless provide us with a wealth of information, sometimes vital, that can greatly assist in dive planning. Firstly, charts provide key information

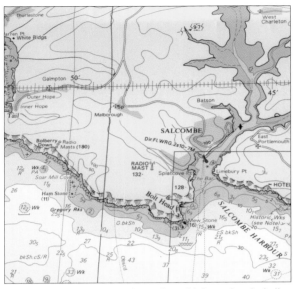

Charts provide divers with a variety of information, including depth and the position of wrecks

An understanding of tides and water depths is essential when using boats

about the depth of the water likely to be encountered at any position. This is normally shown in two ways, by means of depth contour lines (sometimes enhanced by colour) and by means of spot depths. Modern European charts will use metres but in other parts of the world depths marked in feet and fathoms may be found. As the prime purpose of these measurements is to enable safe ship navigation, indicated depths are based on a worst-case scenario, the shallowest water likely to be encountered at that spot. It follows that at most times the actual depth will be greater, principally due to tidal effects. So, unless diving at the shallowest water likely to be encountered at that spot, known as the Lowest Astronomical Tide (LAT), the diver should expect to find deeper water than indicated on the chart, deeper to a degree that may be calculated using data obtainable from tide tables of the area.

Depth contours and chart symbols will enable the dive planner to note the positions of underwater pinnacles and reefs, often also giving some indication of the nature of the sea bed in the area. Among the many symbols used to provide navigational information are those showing the position of shipwrecks, many of which are potential dive sites. Different symbols are used to provide some detail about the actual wreck, such as whether or not any part is above the surface or, if not, the shallowest depth above the wreckage. Many of the symbols are of navigational aids and even in these days of satellite-based GPS (Global Positioning Systems) these buoys, lights and markers can help the diver in position-fixing while making passage or locating the area of a dive site.

Boats

While an equipped diver carrying fins can find firm sand a reasonable surface to walk over, loose dry sand, pebbles and boulders can prove extremely difficult. Unless you are a committed marine biologist, it is worth considering just how interesting you will find exploring a large sandy bay. Generally speaking, rocky ridges that turn into underwater reefs, dramatic cliffs which continue underwater or large boulder fields will provide more underwater life and interest. Shipwrecks are magnets for many forms of underwater life and provide a special attraction for many divers. However, the difficulty with many such sites is that they are not commonly accessible as shore dives.

A day boat with a hoist makes exiting the water easier

A rigid-hull inflatable boat (RIB) provides flexibility in the choice of diving areas

RIBs

This is where our second form of dive site access needs consideration. Boats have long proved popular in transporting divers to those sites without easy land access, so an examination of their planning implications is useful. A first consideration will be how many divers are able to be carried by the various craft. A 5m rigid-hull inflatable boat (RIB) may cope with up to six divers plus a boat handler – any more tends to be a rather a squeeze. RIBs offer higher travel speeds and more comfortable rides but at the price of less room – the centre console takes up a significant amount of inboard space.

Larger RIBs are available, but in diving many of these boats are purchased by clubs and dive centres and they often prefer the flexibility offered by owning two boats. If two or more boats operate together they can offer a higher level of security in covering a dive site besides offering mutual assistance in case of

difficulties, somewhat akin to the diver buddy system.

An advantage with such craft is that they can be launched and recovered fairly easily and towed without too much difficulty to a large range of diving areas. Of course, suitable launch-and-recovery facilities have to be researched but this does provide the diver with an excellent flexibility of dive site choice. As divers are a very easily identifiable part of the community, make sure plenty of consideration is given to the general public when using beaches, ramps or harbours and any launching fees are duly paid.

Day boats

In many areas large day boats are available for hire by specific groups, typically a diving club that might engage the boat and skipper for a weekend or a week's diving. Usually such boats in the UK are

Day boats

Day boats can be hired by groups of divers

licensed to carry a maximum of 12 passengers. Many Mediterranean or tropical dive resorts have larger, often purpose-designed day boats, which depart either once or twice daily visiting a range of dive sites and offering places on a casual basis to any divers. Typically, diving on such a basis will involve diving in a group led by a professional dive leader or guide, unless a prior agreement can be reached with the boat operator for you to dive just with your buddy. If willing, in these circumstances the operator will certainly want evidence of your qualifications and experience and may well insist on a couple of check-out dives with one of their dive leaders.

Liveaboards

Another class of large dive boat is the liveaboard, for many the ultimate in diving luxury. Liveaboards may be purpose-designed and built or converted from some other vessel such as a fishing trawler or a rig-support vessel. They offer the possibility of travelling, sleeping, eating and diving aboard the same platform with the advantage of only having to lug your diving equipment from vehicle to boat and back once per expedition. The range possible from the base port can be pretty extensive, as travel to dive sites can occur overnight or during meal breaks, thus offering a maximum amount and variety of dive sites. Many divers will spend one-week or two-week periods on

Liveaboards allow access to a much wider range of dive sites

such trips, possibly as part of a dive club charter or possibly booking alone or with a dive buddy. With liveaboards available for charter from the North Atlantic to Micronesia and from the Red Sea to the Caribbean, the truly ambitious dive leader is only limited by time and budget.

Obviously the convenience of boat diving has an organisational overhead. There are considerable logistical skills demanded in ensuring everyone is at the departure point with the right equipment and at the right time to enable the boat to be at the dive site for the full period of slack water or whatever other constraints might apply. All the other planning points regarding the provision of dive sites suitable for the experience mix of the group are still valid, as are taking account of water and weather conditions. If the boats are regular diving platforms, entry and exit procedures are not usually a problem but must still be taken into account.

Having gone to the extra effort and expense of organising a boat dive, some time spent on choosing the dive sites is warranted. It would be a shame to use this flexible diving platform just to dive areas accessible as shore dives. Bearing in mind the cruising speed of the dive boat and any time constraints, a range of more adventurous dive sites can be researched from a chart of the locality. Otherwise inaccessible shore sites, offshore islands, pinnacles, reefs and shipwrecks become available. To properly plan and conduct dives on such sites any local knowledge, such as a boat skipper's, will always be valuable. However, sometimes the very nature of the sites may make this difficult and you will have to glean the necessary information from charts and tide tables. Sometimes additional information can also be gathered from books written on diving that region, or from research on the Internet.

Site choice and location

The state of weather, wind and waves will have an important bearing on whether and when a dive is made

Site choice and location

Having covered the planning aspects of site choice we now reach the decision point and we must answer the questions regarding the diving suitability of the site under the current conditions. Are the weather, wind and waves within acceptable limits for those intending to dive the site? Wind direction and current direction can have significant effects on sea conditions. Winds greater than Force 5 will make most coastal sites unsuitable for diving and wave heights that might permit experienced divers to dive safely may be unsuitable for those with lesser experience or may make boat launch sites unusable. What is the forecast for local sea and weather conditions, and have you

allowed plenty of daylight to complete diving operations (cloudy conditions, for instance, can bring darkness forward by a significant period of time)?

Assuming satisfactory answers, we can then proceed to the site location. While some sites can be simply located because they are immediately adjacent to land or visible rocks, many are more difficult to find. Given the small underwater range of a diver, accurate position fixing is crucial. A common method is using visual transits, sightings on a pair of distant objects which provide a sight line that extends to the dive site. Lining up two such sight lines simultaneously can provide a good 'fix' that can often be further verified

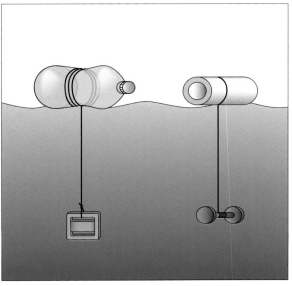

Transits: while stationary in the position you wish to fix, choose two objects which line up. Preferably, these objects should be uniquely obvious and memorable, well separated from each other, have distinct vertical edges and be a point. Your position and these two objects are thus linked by a 'transit' line. Choose at least two and preferably three such transit lines. The intersection of these transit lines fixes your position. If possible, avoid lines at sea level that may change with different states of the tide and try to choose transit lines with around 60° angular separation

Mini-shots: the mini-shot on the left is simple to make up, consisting of a plastic 1-litre drinks bottle fastened to a suitable length of thin line which is wound neatly around it and also attached to a weight. The mini-shot on the right is slightly more sophisticated, comprising a lead bobbin with the line attached and wound around it, the other end of the line is connected to a pre-formed polystyrene can-shaped sleeve in which the lead bobbin is stored. When deployed, the lead bobbin is simply pulled out and the assembly thrown into the water, the polystyrene float then marking the site.

by means of an echosounder. Actual site location is usually performed by driving towards one set of transits and keeping them aligned, until the other transits line up. If available, a GPS fix on a site can be reasonably accurate, with the advantage of it working in areas where good transits are scarce, non-existent or hidden by poor surface visibility. To locate a site using a GPS unit, it is best to arrive in the general area and then use the GPS direction and distance facility to pinpoint the actual site. Ideally, this approach will be made heading into either wind or current, whichever will have the most influence on the boat's handling, a point worth bearing in mind when choosing which line to sail along. An echosounder can often provide confirmation of site location, as well as providing an accurate prediction of the dive depth.

Once the site is reached either the boat will anchor, or will drop off divers and patrol as safety cover. If

the latter then, unless it is a reef or drift dive, it is common to mark the site by means of a shot-line, a subject covered in Chapter Five. For accurate fixing at deep sites, where an approach is made before slack water and some current is still running, it is important that the marker shot sinks as rapidly as possible. For a given weight it is the resistance of the line that will both slow down descent and tend to pull the marker with the current away from the site. Sometimes a mini-shot might be employed in non-tidal conditions, using a weight of around 2kg together with a lightweight (1mm) braided line wound round a floating bobbin. In clear waters this may be sufficient to provide a visual guide for the divers to and even from the site, but care must be taken not to become entangled, and of course it will provide little assistance for in-water decompression.

Global positioning system

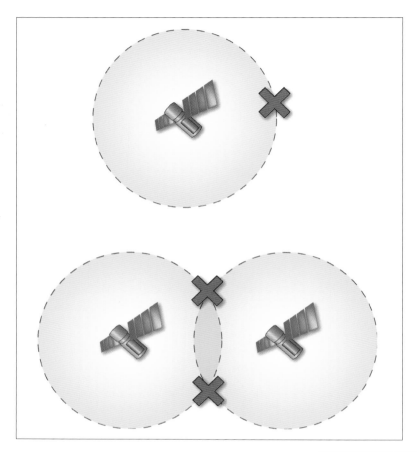

Global Positioning System (GPS)
A constellation of some 24 operational satellites constantly broadcast signals that can be picked up by receivers within their sight line. The receiver can decode this signal to establish both the position of and distance to the satellite. A correctly decoded signal from one satellite means the receiver is somewhere on a sphere of known radius around that satellite. More information will be needed to create a position.

Left, if for simplicity we consider two-dimensional position fixing and regard the satellite signals as providing position circles, then the receiver must be at one of the two points formed by the intersection of two circles.

Right, sticking with the two-dimensional model, given position circles from three satellites enables a unique position fix to be plotted. Of course, we exist in three dimensions so our position is really at the intersection of the radii of three spheres. If we are on the surface of the Earth, then this can be regarded as a fourth sphere and this finally gives us a reasonably accurate fix. A signal from a fourth satellite will enable the receiver to calculate an altitude.

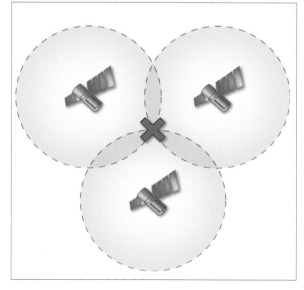

A RIB console including GPS

A handheld GPS

GPS position fixing

Bearing in mind that swimming as a fully kitted diver requires a fair amount of energy and enthusiasm to cover any great distance, most dives cover a fairly small underwater area. Add to this factor the limitations of reduced underwater visibility and you can understand the importance of entering the water as close as possible to the dive target zone. Accurate position fixing when the dive starts, with a reference point showing above the surface, is not too difficult. However, when there are no adjacent surface reference points, position-fixing skills become very important. Fortunately, most dive sites are either within visual range of land or are sufficiently large for modern electronic navigational aids to provide accurate position fixing. Over the last few years the performance of GPS (Global Positioning System) units has developed so rapidly, while at the same time the size and price of the units has reduced, that they have become almost indispensable as a diver's aid to site location.

GPS units depend on access to a selection of a constellation of special earth orbit satellites for their operation. Each satellite broadcasts an extremely accurate time signal based on an atomic clock, which is synchronised to all the other satellites, as well as precise data on its current position. Your GPS receiver can then use the time taken for a signal to travel to it from a given satellite to calculate a distance between the two. The GPS unit contains a mathematical model of the Earth's surface. Using a minimum of three distances measured from three different satellites, the GPS unit can integrate all this information to deduce a very accurate position fix. 'Sight' of more than three satellites can further increase the accuracy of the fix, to the extent that even an altitude can be reported. Currently, units can be purchased which range from wristwatch-sized to console-mounted. They can be stand-alone devices, be incorporated in VHF radios, be add-on units for a handheld or pocket computer (PDA – personal digital assistant) or a laptop computer, or be incorporated in echosounders or other marine electronic instruments. For a diver, having considered the environment it will be used in ('wet' or 'dry' boat), choice will probably be based on factors such as price, position-display method and memory capability. Depending on the model, display can range from a simple latitude and longitude indication to a screen displaying a moving chart image centred on your

Planning for a buddy pair

Making a pre-dive buddy check

A dive briefing on board a day boat

current location. Accuracy is on average around 15m, but with ongoing improvements and new GPS systems coming on line this will reduce significantly.

Besides fixing your current position a number of other useful features may be offered, depending on the model. Virtually all units have the capability of storing 'waypoints', positions such as dive sites that have been previously visited or inserted from chart data or other sources. Any of these waypoints can then be selected as a target destination and the GPS unit will provide a course to steer and a distance to travel. Once travel is underway and a speed is known (calculated directly by the unit) an estimated time of arrival may also be indicated. A GPS unit linked with a PDA or other computer can interact with a database of dive sites and is a powerful aid to dive organisers as the diver can access other stored information on the intended site, such as tidal conditions, wreck details and so on. Diving clubs and individuals are beginning to exchange such data often via the Internet and it is also becoming commercially available from specialist websites.

Planning for a buddy pair

Once the issues of dive site choice and access are resolved and the suitability of the site for the individual divers confirmed, there remains the consideration of the requirements of each buddy pair. The individual divers will need all their usual personal equipment, plus any special equipment demanded by the nature of the planned dive, for example, torches for night dives. In many cases the two divers will have different skill sets and experience levels. Don't forget to check that both skill levels and previous experience are adequate. Obviously they must both have the minimum needed for the planned dive, but it is important that both understand at least the basics of any skills contributed by the other. For example, while it is not expected that a buddy diver will teach an unskilled partner how to use an SMB, the partner should understand the procedures the other diver will be adopting. The leader of the pair will need to agree a dive plan with the buddy and the dive organiser, including details of maximum depth, planned timing and route, decompression, breathing gas and equipment requirements. Once this planning has all been done you are ready for the final briefing, a buddy check and the dive can begin.

A dive marshal takes note of entry and exit times

Dive marshalling

When undertaking any adventurous pursuit, whether it is a land, water or air-centred activity, it is always wise to have some form of back-up in case difficulties are encountered. In recreational diving this is normally covered in two ways. The immediate source of assistance is the diver you are partnered with. In many dives you will be diving as an independent buddy pair, offering each other mutual support whenever needed. Indeed, on many dives the visibility or other underwater conditions mean groups larger than a buddy pair are impracticable and expose the group members to a greater degree of risk. The dive is much more enjoyable if you only need to keep an eye on one other diver, you have more time to enjoy the rest of your surroundings. Some would even argue that diving alone would further increase the enjoyment factor, but in this there is an obvious and dramatic increase in risk that a vast majority

consider unacceptable. In commercial diving the buddy system is normally modified so that while one diver operates alone underwater, a fully equipped and ready-to-dive buddy is on immediate standby at the surface, ready to provide assistance should it be needed. The working diver will be both attached to the surface by a line and have communications with the surface, a far cry from the independence enjoyed by the recreational diver.

A second system of support for divers underwater should be a surface party. While this party can be of variable size, depending on the support any particular diving activity requires, there should be at least one person who is designated as the dive marshal. This is the person who has assessed the site and conditions, understands the intended dive plans of all the diving groups, knows where and at what time they entered the water and where and at what time they should be surfacing again. Knowledge of each diver's underwater autonomy (breathing-gas supply) is also needed. In this way, in the very unlikely event of underwater problems occurring, emergency actions can be initiated without any delay. While extremely rare, there have been odd instances of divers being forgotten by their boat and left with long, distressing swims simply because proper dive marshalling was not conducted. Dive marshals should record details of each diver's entry and exit times, plus maximum depth achieved, as this data is needed in planning subsequent dives. To make this process simpler, reusable pre-printed plastic slates are available which can be conveniently used in wet environments. The data recorded on the slates can then be transcribed to form part of the personal log most divers keep, recording their diving activities.

While acting as dive marshal for a single pair of divers on a shore dive may not be too onerous, performing the same duty for a sizeable party diving offshore will be a different matter. Either a large boat or possibly a group of smaller boats could be used as the diving platform and it is likely that more than one dive group will need to be underwater at the same time. If the tidal window is small, timings will be very tight. Overall, a lot of organisation is called for and both effective management and good communication skills are essential. The dive marshal must be in overall charge of the diving activities, controlling when individual divers enter the water, having verified with boat skipper or coxswain that propellers are stationary. Managing large groups of divers will call for delegation of some tasks, particularly in the case of a number of smaller dive boats working together. It is usual for the dive marshal to have the final say in all matters of safety, deciding whether the prevailing conditions are suitable for each diver or buddy pair.

Risk assessment

Risk assessment has always been an inherent part of properly organised diving and diver training. Currently there is pressure, especially in commercial operations, to formally record certain elements of this process in a form accepted by health and safety officials. Although as an activity diving is high in potential hazards, the accident rate is low compared with most other adventurous pursuits, coming well below even horse riding, and in these terms has been likened to normal car driving. This is primarily because good dive planning incorporates a

large element of risk assessment. In identifying hazards it is helpful to focus on who might be injured in specific situations. Analysis should take into account such parameters as the site, prevailing conditions, the equipment being used, the capabilities of the divers and the planned dive activity. Once the hazards are known, the consequential severity of each one can be judged and the chance of occurrence can be considered, to provide an overall assessment of risk. This can then be set against a suitable preventative control to be adopted to minimise the risk and an evaluation of the safety of the situation can be made.

Hazard	Risk level	Controls	Planned reaction
Ruptured eardrum	low	Ear clearing, descent control	Immediate ascent, buddy assistance, medical check
Decompression illness	medium	Planning with tables/computer, monitoring exposure, slow controlled ascent	Therapeutic oxygen, emergency evacuation to recompression facility
Nitrogen narcosis	high	Progressive depth increments, experienced buddy	Immediate ascent, buddy assistance

Risk level				
	Injury level			
	minor	moderate	major	fatal
Frequent	medium	high	high	high
Occasional	low	medium	high	high
Rare	low	low	medium	high

Examples of specific hazards to a member of a dive group and of standard risk analysis can be seen in the charts opposite. Provided such analysis is a feature of your dive planning, you should enjoy dives which although high in potential hazard will be low in actual risk. However, good risk assessment is a continuous process and should not end with the dive planning stage. A sensible diver will carefully monitor dive progress and continuously apply risk assessment principles to the conduct of the dive.

Are you healthy enough to dive?

Divers are intially medically assessed before starting a dive-training programme. As a dive leader you are extending your diving abilities and will also be concerned with the health of those you will be diving with. The medical suitability of most recreational divers is today ascertained by self-completion of a questionnaire, although a few countries still require examination by a medical practitioner. Whichever method is used, the areas examined are similar, concentrating on circulatory and respiratory function and body parts with air-filled cavities such as the ears and nasal passages. Certain diseases are often regarded as disqualifying, as too are some post-disease or trauma effects such as perforated eardrums or types of lung scarring. Many authorities have now abandoned invasive screening techniques such as chest x-rays and prefer MRI scans if referral indicates a more detailed examination is called for.

If the assessment is carried out by means of a self-declaration questionnaire or a non-diving specialist doctor, doubtful areas may need to be explored further through consultation with a doctor specialising in diving medicine. This is because certain medical conditions are regarded as being marginally allowable or allowable subject to restrictions of depth or other diving conditions. Be aware that day-to-day changes in your health may well affect your suitability to dive. Diving while undergoing medication also requires serious consideration as the effects of the medication may vary under pressure, or may serve to mask symptoms of decompression illness (DCI). Oral contraceptives and diuretics are generally considered allowable, and antihistamines and analgesics under caution. Use of psychotropic drugs (including tranquillisers, sedatives and hypnotics) is of particular concern and expert advice should be sought from a qualified diving-

Exercise tolerance test are sometimes used in evaluating the health of professional dive leaders

Diving and the law

medicine specialist. Most medical authorities counsel against diving during pregnancy, as the effects of pressure and changed gas partial pressures on a foetus are unknown. Smoking is counselled against as it predisposes the smoker to air embolism, pneumothorax and coronary thrombosis, besides reducing general fitness. High blood pressure should also be a concern requiring expert advice and may well be a disqualifying condition.

Today, recreational diving is accessible to people with a wide range of conditions previously considered as disallowable factors. A number of clubs, organisations and schools provide specialist support for people with disabilities who wish to dive.

Diabetes was once considered a diving contra-indicator, but certain classes of this condition are now allowed by some organisations, subject to medical supervision and other limitations.

Travelling divers may encounter problems as different medical screening systems apply in different countries, some still requiring a certificate validated by a medical practitioner and some even insisting on a local examination. Make sure you travel with any appropriate certification you possess. Working (remunerated) dive leaders (and instructors) often come under a different set of regulations to those applicable to the ordinary recreational diver. Often they will be required to undergo a thorough examination, usually annually renewable, by an approved diving medicine practitioner. Such examinations can be expensive, requiring procedures such as MRI scans and exercise tolerance tests.

Diving and the law

While you will not encounter patrolling underwater police on every dive, there is nevertheless a body of law affecting the diver. This legislation is designed to both protect our underwater world and ourselves as divers, covering environmental issues, equipment safety and training standards. Before you even enter the water you need to be aware of the regulations concerning the equipment you are using. A diving cylinder filled to its working pressure is effectively a vast energy store and if faulty or mistreated can either explode or be violently propelled by escaping high-pressure gas. Consequently, most countries have legislation setting out a periodic testing programme and safe transport procedures for such containers. All European countries follow the various procedures laid down by the CEN (Comité Européen de Normalisation) standards body, so it is wise to be familiar with whatever the current standards require. CEN also publishes standards for many other types of equipment used in diving, but here it is the manufacturer and supplier that must comply with the standards. Other CEN standards apply to the training programmes offered to divers, to diving instructors and to diving service providers. Worldwide, most countries have regulations concerning dive cylinders and a number of countries have regulations covering breathing gases.

Access to the water is also frequently subject to rules and regulations. The land bordering the water will be owned by individuals, private organisations or public authorities who may or may not allow divers rights to enter or exit the water, and in some cases the water itself may also be owned. Make sure you are not committing trespass, follow any local requirements and pay any dues. With all our equipment we often need vehicular access and parking can cause problems. Besides being sure to park legally, make sure you are not obstructing access to any site by others, especially emergency services.

Before entering the water there are further regulatory considerations. A number of countries are happy to allow anyone to dive but many have certain training or health prerequisites. This may be a simple self declaration of medical fitness to dive, or may require a medical certificate from a suitably qualified doctor, possibly even including a chest x-ray. The type of dive (including depth limitations) you are permitted to make may even be legally governed by your training level. France, Spain and Malta are particular examples of countries where such regulations can be encountered. Countries frequently impose much tighter controls as soon as there is any commercial activity involved, such as a diving school or remunerated underwater work.

Once in the water you have not escaped the long arm of the law. Most countries have strict laws governing all kinds of fishing and as a diver you are not exempt. In some cases, limited fishing is allowed with a suitable licence, usually with restrictions on seasons and size of catch. Be aware that in most cases such regulations also apply to the taking of shellfish. Laws notwithstanding, regard for underwater conservation and respect for the sensibilities of local professional fishermen usually

Most countries have strict laws and regulations that apply to the taking of shellfish

Legislation applies to the recovery of any artefacts

demand divers abstain from removing any marine life. As mentioned earlier, working underwater for any kind of pecuniary reward is usually the subject of very strict control, normally demanding professional diving qualifications. A high level of surface support is also frequently demanded and regulated. The term 'underwater work' in this sense can include tasks such as clearing propellers or searching for and recovering lost objects if any kind of payment is made for the service.

Another body of legislation applies to the discovery and recovery of objects found underwater. In most countries there is a legal requirement to report the discovery of any historic artefacts. Disturbing or recovering such objects is usually forbidden without a special licence and in many cases contravention of such regulations can not only result in fines or prison sentences, but also loss of all diving equipment possibly extending to boats and other vehicles involved. Where historic underwater sites are identified frequently the area becomes a legally protected zone where diving is either closely regulated or even forbidden.

Besides the protection of archaeological sites, there are also many laws covering the loss of ships and

their cargoes. In some cases complex rules apply, differentiating between:

- **jetsam:** objects deliberately jettisoned to try to prevent a ship sinking
- **flotsam:** objects floating away from a sinking vessel
- **lagan:** objects jettisoned but buoyed for later recovery
- **wreck:** generally wreckage cast ashore but also may be applied to the shipwreck itself.

However, the underlying principle is that all of these objects have legal owners or are subject to legal procedures and any diver wishing to take possession or otherwise recover such objects must follow the requirements of the law.

Bear in mind that even objects recovered outside a country's territorial waters usually come under these same laws when landed. Current thinking is that the best advice is to look but don't touch and most diving organisations recommend adherence to a wreck diver's Code of Conduct. ◻

Chapter two

The diving environment

Weather conditions and the environment in which you intend to dive are crucial factors to take into account when planning your dives. The state of the tide, temperature and weather will all have a bearing on whether or not you dive, when you dive and the type of diving you are likely to undertake. A freshwater site will have considerable differences to a saltwater one, and you should be able to act and plan appropriately for each different dive.

The diving environment
Tides

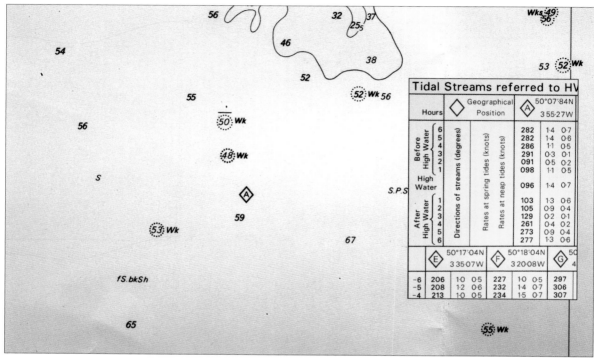

Tidal Streams referred to HW					
Hours	◇ Geographical Position	◬ A 50°07'.84N 3 55.27W	Directions of streams (degrees)	Rates at spring tides (knots)	Rates at neap tides (knots)
Before High Water 6			282	1.4	0.7
5			282	1.4	0.6
4			286	1.1	0.5
3			291	0.3	0.1
2			091	0.5	0.2
1			098	1.1	0.5
High Water			096	1.4	0.7
After High Water 1			103	1.3	0.6
2			105	0.9	0.4
3			129	0.2	0.1
4			261	0.4	0.2
5			273	0.9	0.4
6			277	1.3	0.6

	◬ E 50°17'.04N 3 35.07W			◬ F 50°18'.04N 3 20.08W			◬ G 5C...
-6	206	1.0	0.5	227	1.0	0.5	297
-5	208	1.2	0.6	232	1.4	0.7	306
-4	213	1.0	0.5	234	1.5	0.7	307

On charts, tidal diamonds are used – along with a related table – to indicate the state of tides

Tides

A knowledge of tidal movements is vital when dive planning. Those intent on dive leading will need to become familiar with the impact that tidal flows and cycles have on a dive and this will require an understanding of how to read charts.

At various points on the majority of charts you can find a purple diamond shape with a letter inside it. These are known as tidal diamonds. Elsewhere on the chart, usually in an area where it will not obscure important navigational detail, there will be a table relating the tidal current to be expected at the position of the diamond, with tide times at a local reference port. Armed with a tide table for that port, you can then easily work out the expected current speed and direction at any particular time. Careful study of the table will allow you to see at what time the current slows and then reverses direction. It is around this time that you can expect to find a 'window' of slack water that will provide the most comfortable diving. As you are unlikely to be diving precisely where the tidal diamond is positioned on the chart, you will have to find the nearest and then also look at any others in the vicinity to interpolate data on currents for your chosen site. Local geography can also have a significant effect on timing, as shallow ground or nearby islands can advance or delay the actual time of slack water at a particular site. It is wise to obtain as much local knowledge as possible and to arrive early at the site and watch for the time when the current slacks off enough to provide comfortable diving conditions.

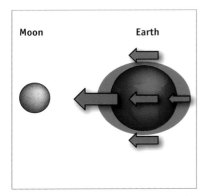

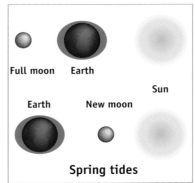

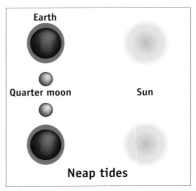

The main influence on our oceans is the gravitational force of the Earth. This is modified by the smaller gravitational force of the moon to produce a tidal effect. As the earth rotates a point on the surface will experience two high water levels in each rotation

Although larger, the greater distance of the sun means its gravitational tidal effect is less than that of the moon. If the two are acting in a line, as above, the tidal effect is greater producing higher high and lower low tides. These occur every two weeks and are referred to as Spring tides

When the sun and the moon are at right angles (in 'quadrature'), their gravitational forces conflict and so produce a smaller tidal effect. These tides are called Neap tides

In the North Atlantic, frequently this slack-water window will be rather short, typically between 20 and 40 minutes. This means divers will often have to start the dive as the current slows in one direction, but will surface as the tide picks up and runs in the opposite direction. Remember that tides are caused by the rotation of the earth and the relative positions of the earth, sun and moon, all of which are constantly changing, though fortunately in a predictable manner. As the earth rotates each 25 hours or so, the North Atlantic experiences two high and two low tides – that is, two complete tidal cycles. Note that because the sun and moon are not stationary, the cycle is longer than our simple 24-hour temporal day. At each tidal flow reversal we will have a period of slack water. Obviously, diving at the slack water period nearest low water will give a certain depth advantage as the shallower water means that there is a lower decompression penalty.

During each lunar month, due to the relative positions of the sun and moon, there is a cycle of increasing and then decreasing tidal flow superimposed on the normal daily tide. This gives two periods of stronger (Spring) tides some two weeks apart and two periods of weaker (Neap) tides spaced between them. As tidal flows are greater during Spring tides which occur just after a full or new moon, this is when the largest tides and strongest currents will be experienced. Conversely, if diving can be planned around the Neap tides, just after the first or last quarter lunar periods, weaker tides and currents, and longer slack-water windows will be found. Tidal flows are also affected by the size and shape of the body of water, so producing quite large tidal ranges in some areas and virtually none in others. The Atlantic coasts of northern Europe experience quite large tides while Mediterranean coasts have small tidal ranges. Coastal shaping even produces a tidal flow in the Solent, a body of water between the Isle of Wight and the South Coast, giving four instead of two tide cycles per day, making for some challenging dive-planning.

Currents are not always something divers seek to avoid. Properly planned and supported drift dives (see Chapter Six) can be exhilarating and enable a large underwater area to be observed in a single dive, though not always in great detail!

The weather has an important effect on the condition of the sea

Wind over tide creates a choppy surface

Weather

As weather can have such an important effect on both underwater and surface conditions, good dive planning demands a basic competence in at least interpreting the weather forecast information. This may be obtained from general broadcasts or the Internet, but is likely to be more detailed from local sources such as harbourmasters, marinas or coastguards. Dive planning involves a considerable amount of effort, so it is always wise to have contingency plans should adverse weather arrive. Shore diving where there are headlands or islands can often mean that alternative sites may be located nearby. If an onshore wind creates unpleasant wave action, then the lee side of the headland or island may provide calm and sheltered conditions that are perfectly diveable. Beware that venturing too far out on the surface can quickly remove you from this shelter and create the hazard of an offshore wind, blowing you away from safety.

Weather forecasting is a complex topic. On land, we spend our lives at the bottom of a vast and turbulent atmosphere which is constantly in motion. By comparison the sea we dive in is a viscous and sluggish medium that moves around only in slow motion. The atmosphere is a mixture of gases and water, the water being mainly vapour, and the action of the water evaporating and condensing plays a major role in the enormous energy exchanges that power the Earth's weather systems. For divers the most significant aspect of a weather system is usually the strength and direction of associated winds.

As the wind blows across the surface of the sea, friction between the air and the water causes turbulence in both – this being visible as waves. The longer and stronger the wind blows, the larger these waves can become, especially far out in the oceans where there are no surface obstructions to modify or slow down the wind. The effect of these storms far out in the ocean can cause long swells in waters hundreds of miles distant, swells that can seriously affect diving close to exposed shorelines. Generally these are conditions that worsen (and improve) over a timescale that should not cause difficulties to observant divers. It is usually more local weather systems that cause most problems. If there is a current moving the water in the same direction as the wind is blowing, the effective wind speed over the water is reduced and wave

Our watery globe

A diver inspects some of the prolific marine life found in temperate waters

generation is lower. There can be a speeding up of the water movement that can affect slack water timing and duration. On the other hand, if the water flow and air flow are in opposite directions, a nasty short chop can quickly build up and diving and boating conditions rapidly become uncomfortable.

Other weather phenomena that can affect divers are those involving changed surface visibility. Sudden rain squalls can quickly reduce surface visibility and are often accompanied by winds that create a nasty chop to the water making it difficult to spot surfacing divers. Mist and fog can create similar diver recovery problems. With satellite observation and measurement, weather forecasting today can often be pleasingly accurate, especially for short-term forecasts. Make sure before setting out for a dive that you have as accurate a picture of the likely weather conditions as is possible and that you keep a careful watch on any changes. Get up-to-date information from local

sources such as the coastguard or local harbourmaster. Also, pay careful attention to any threatening cloud formations that may indicate localised squalls or other weather deterioration.

Our watery globe

While it is useful to divide the world into conventional zones defined by latitude, colder in the polar regions and hotter as the equator is approached, it must be remembered that there are areas that are atypical largely because of the effects of major oceanic currents. The Mediterranean and much of the northwest coasts of Scotland and Norway are examples of such areas. In the southern hemisphere the periodic ice limits extend into most of the lower fifties latitudes. In the northern hemisphere, southeast Canada, Siberia and Hokkaido – which are in the mid forties latitude – are also affected by these ice limits, while Iceland, Norway

Diving in polar waters requires specific thermal protection

Inland dive sites offer divers a different set of conditions to deal with

and even the west coast of Spitzbergen at almost 80° remain ice free. These climatic effects obviously have an effect on the underwater flora and fauna, the diver will encounter and will also influence the training requirements and equipment needs of the diver.

Temperate zone

Covering the Atlantic coasts of western Europe, western Canada and the USA, South Africa, much of South America, Japan, Korea, China and Australia and New Zealand, the economic structure of the world dictates that these are the home waters of most recreational divers. In UK waters alone it is estimated that some four million recreational dives are made each year. With water temperatures generally ranging between 10 and 25°C, diving tends to be seasonal in both drysuits and wetsuits. Underwater life is prolific and varied and visibility is also very variable, often changing with the seasons as plankton blooms occur. Because of the long history of economic development and the many wars that have centred on a number of these regions, they are rich in shipwrecks. Weather, tide and current often have a strong influence on diving.

Polar regions

Proportionately very little recreational diving takes place in polar waters, most diving activity being undertaken by scientists, particularly marine biologists. Conditions are extreme, with both thermal insulation and equipment performance being major issues. In stark contrast to the 12-hour day and 12-hour night of the equator, dramatic seasonal daylight variations are experienced, with daylight varying from virtually 24 hours to almost none as the seasons change. Remoteness from back-up support, transportation and communication difficulties are further problems for polar divers to resolve. Diving demands the support of a well planned, equipped and staffed expedition.

Lakes and rivers

With many divers living a long way from the sea, a great deal of diving, especially training dives, takes place in a variety of inland sites, varying from flooded quarries to lakes, canals and rivers. Some of these areas are small seas and some hardly more than a pond. The fact is if the water is diveable some diver will want to dive there. All these sites have something to offer the adventurous diver, whether it be the experience

A wreck dive in the Mediterranean

of diving at altitude, the freshwater flora and fauna, a search for old bottles beside a canalside pub or just a convenient local training spot. With most of these sites being fresh water, there is an added advantage in that rinsing equipment afterwards is much easier. Surface temperatures vary with climatic zone, season and altitude. In larger bodies of water thermoclines are usual with water below 20m a cold and static 4°C all year round. Variable visibility is likely with silt being a common problem. In contrast, though, certain sites (often subterranean) are renowned for their crystal-clear conditions.

The Mediterranean

The cradle of recreational diving, the Mediterranean is a global special case. Its relatively warm, clear waters and negligible tidal movement together with its proximity to so many European divers have long made it a prime dive target. Sadly, a history of pollution and over-fishing have over recent years diminished its popularity, especially when set against the current availability of cheap package tours to the Red Sea, Thailand and the Maldives. Some Mediterranean countries have belatedly set up underwater reserves with commercial fishing and recreational spear fishing forbidden in an attempt to reverse the almost complete disappearance of large territorial fish. Most diving is performed in the warmer Spring, Summer and Autumn months with divers generally using semi-drysuits and thinner 5mm suits.

Tropical zone

Because of the pleasant water temperatures most of the world's most popular dive sites are to be found in the Tropics. Festooned with coral reefs populated by some of the planet's most exotic and colourful marine life, several millions of recreational dives are made in these areas every year. The Australian Great Barrier reef must be one of the world's most well known diving attractions, but in sheer numbers of dives Florida, the Bahamas and the islands of the Caribbean take some beating. Mexico, Sri Lanka, the islands of the Indian Ocean, Melanesia, Micronesia and Polynesia all provide world-class tropical diving and include among them some areas ripe for exploration and development. For European divers the Red Sea is probably the most economically accessible tropical

The coral reefs of the Tropics attract large numbers of divers

dive spot, with Thailand starting to challenge its position. Malaysia and the Philippines, and to a lesser extent Indonesia and Papua New Guinea, attract large numbers of divers from South East Asia, the most numerous diving tourists being the Japanese.

The warm, clear waters of the Tropics make learning to dive with the minimum of equipment a cheap and attractive proposition for tens of thousands of tourists each year. Many of these tourists become addicted to diving tropical waters, returning time after time and continuing their underwater adventure at the same basic level. Protective clothing is often worn only for comfort and abrasion protection with only minimal thermal protection needed even at a depth of 30m. Because all that many divers seek are underwater guided tours, there is a sizeable employment market for dive leaders, but be warned – one of the attractions of the diving is the low cost and that is reflected in the low pay. Fortunately for the dive leader, living costs in a tropical paradise are also proportionately lower. ☐

Chapter three

Breathing gas

For those new to the sport, breathing gas usually means 'air', and the type of diving done at this entry level means long decompression stops are not required. However, as you grow in experience your diving is likely to become more adventurous and will demand that you pay even closer attention to the effects of nitrogen and the pertinent safety procedures required to deal with increased exposure to it. More advanced divers might make use of alternative breathing gases such as Nitrox and Trimix, both of which have specific training needs.

Breathing gas
Consumption rate

Monitoring a dive's progress

Once the dive site and target depth are known, an important part of dive planning is ensuring sufficient breathing gas will be available to the diver. A range of factors is involved in ensuring this will be so, such as the size of the dive cylinder, the pressure to which it has been charged and the air-consumption rate of the diver. This air-consumption rate will in turn depend upon the depths at which the dive will be conducted and the physical effort being expended, such as finning or other underwater work. Experience, fitness, water temperature, anxiety and body size are also likely to influence a diver's breathing rate. For relatively inexperienced divers, an assumed surface equivalent breathing rate of 25 litres per minute is often used. As your number of logged dives increases,

by noting your cylinder size, dive start and end pressures and dive depth and time profiles, you can gain a more accurate idea of your personal breathing characteristics in different diving conditions. A more reasonable breathing rate used by many experienced relaxed divers is 15 litres per minute. Two nomograms based on these two rates are provided as appendices (see Appendix Five) to take the number crunching out of this area of dive planning. In order to calculate air requirements, multiply your breathing rate by your time at a particular depth, then multiply the result by the ambient pressure at that depth. To calculate ambient pressure use the equation: (depth / 10m) + 1 bar. This calculation can be performed for all sections of the dive, generally with an allowance for ascent and

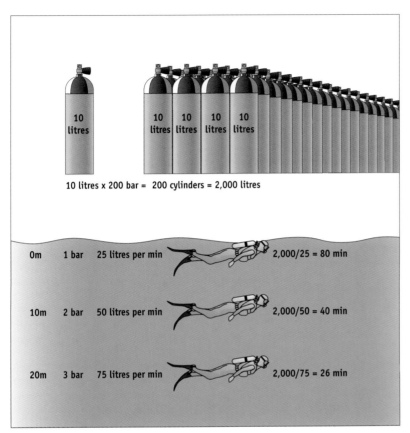

10 litres x 200 bar = 200 cylinders = 2,000 litres

0m	1 bar	25 litres per min		2,000/25 = 80 min
10m	2 bar	50 litres per min		2,000/50 = 40 min
20m	3 bar	75 litres per min		2,000/75 = 26 min

Left, for dive planning a diver must know how much breathing gas is available

Below, always keep an appropriate reserve of breathing gas for the planned dive

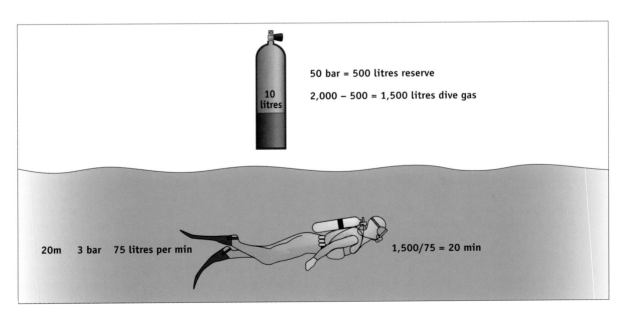

50 bar = 500 litres reserve

2,000 – 500 = 1,500 litres dive gas

| 20m | 3 bar | 75 litres per min | | 1,500/75 = 20 min |

Consumption rate

descent time being included (as time at depth) and so the air to be consumed on the dive can be quantified. For safety, a reserve must be added to this amount and the amount of this reserve may vary depending on the nature of the dive. Generally speaking, the more serious the dive the more generous this reserve will need to be. For simple recreational dives many people plan to reach the surface with between 300 and 500 litres of reserve breathing gas. With a cylinder size of 10 litres, this would correspond to a contents gauge reading of between 30 and 50 bar. The actual amount of breathing gas available from the cylinder is simply calculated by multiplying the cylinder size (how much water you could pour into it) by its charged pressure. Similarly, the air consumed during a dive is the difference between the start and finish dive-cylinder pressures multiplied by the cylinder size.

Should something go wrong with your buddy's equipment towards the end of the dive, the reserve you have calculated for yourself may be inadequate to get both of you back to the surface. Therefore, prudent divers carry an independent back-up emergency gas supply consisting of a pony cylinder with its own regulator. The pony cylinder's size can vary from three to seven litres, but it needs to contain an adequate gas supply to enable the user to regain the surface, including any decompression obligations, from the most critical point of the dive.

The more advanced the dive, the more detailed the breathing-gas-requirement planning will need to be. For deep diving or no-clear surface diving, a useful technique is to adopt a 'rule of thirds'. The amount of breathing gas needed to reach the most extreme part of the dive is calculated as explained above. This quantity is then multiplied by three to obtain the gas needed for the dive, so giving one third for achieving the target, one third for the return and one third for ascent and reserve.

A further complication on more advanced dives will be calculating the breathing gas needed for any in-water decompression stops. As depths and times are predictable, the calculations are not too onerous, but they must, of course, not be forgotten.

Decompression

The basic knowledge about gas absorption and release by body tissues during diving and the resultant problems encountered by decompressing divers has already been covered in earlier training. It is important to realise that there is no such thing as a no-decompression dive. All dives involve compression, which causes extra gas to be absorbed by the body tissues. It follows that at some stage the dive will end with a return to surface pressure and this part is therefore a decompression process. When a decrease of pressure occurs, the excess gas absorbed during the compression phase of the dive will start to be released. Typically, the compression phase of the dive tends to be the longest, the ascent pressure-release part being relatively short. So it is normal for the diver to spend much more time underwater absorbing gas rather than releasing it, arriving back at the surface with an excess of gas still in the body tissues. As long as the ascent is suitably slow and controlled and the amount of excess gas not too great, this is not a problem. Research has indicated that certain levels of excess gas can be tolerated without ill effect. Provided these levels are not exceeded, a normal ascent may be made to the surface. If absorbed levels of gas in the diver's body tissues are too great, the diver will need to stop at a relatively shallow depth (around 6m) to allow excess gas to be released via the bloodstream and the lungs. If this in-water 'stop' is omitted there is a real danger of physical damage occurring, damage which could be fatal, so an understanding of this topic is crucial.

The ratios of various time and depth combinations allowing direct ascents are expressed in decompression tables. While these are sometimes misleadingly called 'no-decompression' dives, they are more correctly identified as 'no-in-water-stop' dives. This is often shortened to 'no-stop' dive, but this does ignore the fact that all dives involve a 'decompression' stop.

Where no in-water stop is required there will always be a period on the surface when off-gassing is occurring until normal atmospheric pressure saturation levels are attained. This period is effectively a decompression stop, with change of pressure constraints being placed on the diver in terms of follow-on dives or ascents to altitude until such time as the excess gas has dissipated from the body tissues. Most decompression tables also provide advice on how to conduct successive dives during these 'surface' stops and on flying or otherwise ascending to altitude.

Divers decompressing on a trapeze

Decompression

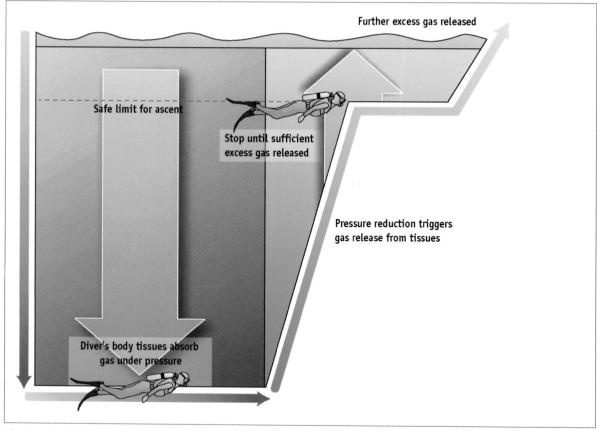

Dive duration and depth combine to affect the gas load absorbed in a diver's body tissues. The ascent phase must be controlled t allow a safe release of this gas load.

As longer and deeper dives are made, the amount of gas absorbed can be sufficient to preclude a direct ascent to the surface, requiring a stop to be made in shallower water until a proportion of the excess gas is released. Such constraints are often referred to as a 'ceiling', where there is a specific depth limitation on the diver's ascent. Ascents involving obligatory stops are referred to as 'staged' ascents and again the decompression tables indicate the depths and durations of such in-water stops.

Dive computers will also provide the necessary data and advice on decompression requirements, often giving useful extra indicators such as ascent speed. Dive management using a modern dive computer is much simpler, more effective and safer than in the old watch and depth gauge days, as long as the diver has the knowledge and ability to understand and use the information provided. While a decompression computer is the most accurate depth and time monitor divers have yet had available, it is important to recognise that the information it provides is guidance.

A computer's use is not intended to replace ultimate decision-making, control or dive conduct responsibility from the diver. Don't switch off your thinking when the dive computer switches on! Unless the underlying principles of compression and decompression are understood, neither tables nor computer will enable a diver to safely plan and control his or her dives.

Decompression terminology

Any decompression table is in fact a compilation of dives using a maximum exposure time and depth to indicate a safe ascent procedure back to surface pressure. In order to quantify this process, a number of parameters have to be measured and so defined:

- **Depth:** the maximum depth attained during the dive
- **Descent rate:** the speed at which the diver descends, typically with a maximum of 30m per minute
- **Bottom time:** originally the time spent at the deepest depth, but often taken to be the time elapsed from the start of the dive to the beginning of the ascent
- **Dive time:** the elapsed time from the start of the dive to arrival at either 6m or the first decompression stop
- **Dive duration:** total time immersed
- **Ascent time:** a dive planning term, used to indicate a time to depart from depth to attain a target arrival time at a decompression stop.
- **Ascent rate:** depending on the table used, either a target ascent speed or an ascent speed limit. Typically in the range of 18m to 6m per minute, often being slower as depth decreases and the surface approaches
- **Surfacing code:** usually an alphabetical code which describes the degree of saturation of a diver's body tissues at the end of a dive
- **Surface interval:** the time spent at surface ambient pressure between two dives
- **Decompression stop:** the process of maintaining a particular depth for a set time period to allow sufficient tissue off-gassing for a further ascent to be made
- **No-stop dive:** a dive that does not require an in-water staged stop during the ascent
- **Decompression stop dive:** a dive that does require an in-water staged stop during the ascent
- **Repeat or successive dive:** a dive where the body tissues have a residual saturation level that will affect this second or successive dive.

A dive conduct slate

Altitude and pressure changes

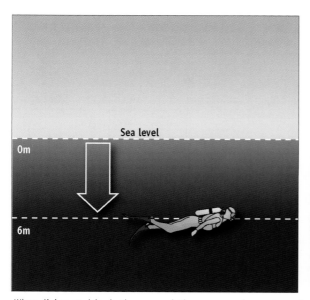 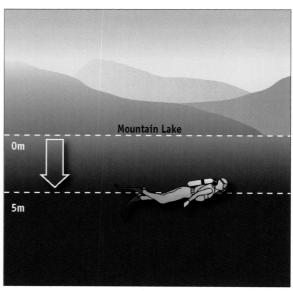

When diving at altitude the same relative pressure change is produced by a smaller depth change

Altitude and pressure changes

Successful decompression practice means solving the reduction in pressure on body tissues containing elevated levels of dissolved gas. The reduction in pressure is normally caused by an ascent through the water, but this is not a linear process. The nearer the diver gets to the surface, the greater the rate of change of pressure. Besides the velocity of the ascending diver, the actual values for this rate of change depend on the density of the water and the atmospheric pressure the diver will exit into. For practical purposes the water density can be regarded as unchanging, but that is far from being the case for the atmospheric pressure. It is well known that atmospheric pressure reduces with rising altitude, but it is also true that local air pressure is significantly affected by changing weather conditions. These changes can have an important effect on the decompression requirements for any given dive. If the ambient pressure where the dive terminates is lower than normal sea-level atmospheric pressure, then the relative pressure change the diver experiences on ascent will be increased. In turn, such an increase in pressure change will be more provocative in bubble formation and will increase the risk of decompression illness (DCI). This demands that adjustments will need to be made to our decompression procedures when diving under such conditions and highlights that it is more important to know the ambient exit pressure rather than simply the dive site altitude.

Traditional tables presumed all dives terminated in a standard atmospheric pressure. If divers wished to dive in bodies of water at altitude, a very crude mathematical adjustment to the decompression table was made. No account was taken of diving under reduced ambient pressures, such as low-pressure weather systems. Today, better tables are available which provide detailed, easy-to-use solutions to diving under a variety of surface pressures, allowing simple dive planning and conduct both at altitude and at sea level when low-pressure weather systems occur. Similarly, good dive computers are programmed to measure and take into account the prevailing ambient pressure. Typically adaptations will include lengthened and possibly deeper in-water stops and lengthened surface interval times.

Decompression ambiguities

When interpreting any decompression situation which raises doubts, the worst case should always be assumed. In tables, if your target depth is not shown take the next deeper increment. Similarly, decompress for the time entry longer than your time – not shorter! Remember, it is far better to curtail an interesting dive and survive to do another one than to suffer DCI and possibly never dive again.

Mixing flying and diving

Most divers will at some time be affected by the question of exposure to lower ambient pressure following a dive. Flying home after a diving holiday is a typical example of this situation, but it can also occur at any time after diving if a journey involves an increase in altitude. This could be using any mode of transport, including by foot! Changing weather conditions alone, such as the arrival of a depression, will not usually be a real problem because of the timescale involved. The body tissues are still off-loading excess gas in the period immediately following a dive and this should effectively be regarded as a decompression stop. If the diver proceeds to a lower ambient pressure, during this period there will be a risk of decompression illness as this is effectively the same as rising above an in-water decompression depth before the stop is finished. Until gas tissue loadings are adequately reduced, therefore, it is vital that divers remain at the same atmospheric pressure.

When an aircraft takes off and rises to cruising altitude there is a swift drop in air pressure which is thought to commonly result in the formation of normally asymptomatic micro-bubbles in the occupants' bloodstreams. For divers part-way through a decompression process this could obviously be the trigger that provokes DCI, so it is important that they do not to expose themselves to this risk. Generally speaking, after a 16-hour surface interval divers are considered sufficiently off-gassed to fly, but many prefer the additional security of waiting for 24 hours before flying.

Divers who have been exposed to low-pressure situations before diving do not normally have any problems to overcome. In fact, the exposure will result in a lowering of dissolved gas in the tissues before the dive, so is probably beneficial. This presumed benefit

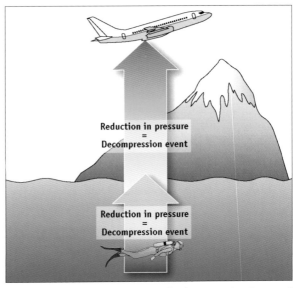

Flying too soon after a dive increases the chances of decompression illness

could arise by taking a long flight or living at a higher altitude than the dive site. However, a short flight may create a penalty rather than a benefit. This is because the micro-bubbles triggered as a result of the ascent phase of the flight may still be present for up to 90 minutes. Should the aircraft land before this time it is possible that sufficient micro-bubbles could still be present and so modify gas uptake during a subsequent dive. To be sure that this effect is fully accounted for, it is wise to wait ten hours following any flight of less than 90 minutes or to apply shorter decompression limits on your dive.

Sawtooth profiles

Yo-yo(or sawtooth)dive profile.
To be avoided

Dive ascents can provoke micro-bubbles which may be compressed and pass into the arterial circulation on subsequent descents

Sawtooth dive profiles

Dive profiles with repetitive descents and ascents are not advised, primarily because during the ascents micro-bubbles can be created in the venous blood and can then build up in the lung capillaries. When a re-descent is made in this situation, the additional pressure could reduce the size of the bubbles appreciably to allow them to pass through the lung capillary bed and into the arterial circulation. In this situation the micro-bubbles could then lodge in arterial capillaries further downstream and cut off blood supply to vital tissues by acting as an embolism (blood clot). All steps must be taken to reduce the potential ill effects of the sometimes unavoidable ascents and re-descents which, in practice, might take place during diving. Try to keep the variation to less than 6m and make any such event as near to the beginning of diving as possible when the gas-tissue loads are minimal. Towards the end of the dive, when gas loads are greater, re-descents are likely to be more risky. Also hazardous are variations at shallow depths where the comparative pressure gradients are steeper. With variations of more than 6m it is prudent to implement conservative decompression strategies.

An extreme example of a sawtooth profile would be diver separation resulting in ascending to the surface, re-grouping and then re-descending. Any continuation of diving activity in this case must be treated as a second dive.

Ascent speed

Practical techniques for measuring ascent rate when diving free from surface control are few and the need for good initial training cannot be over-emphasised. Gaining an early awareness of speed judgement by performing carefully timed ascents from particular depths, with a visual reference such as a shot-line, is important experience. A careful choice of depths will minimise the need for mathematics underwater, and other ascent procedures (such as checking on your buddy) should not be forgotten.

Safety stops

A number of authorities on diving have long encouraged the practice of a 'safety' stop as a precaution on dives where the table allows a direct return to the surface. Making a three-minute stop on

Making a safety stop

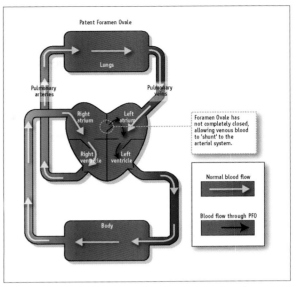

Some 25 per cent of the population may have a PFO

dives, particularly where maximum depths of 30m or more have been reached, is often sensible and has the advantage of taking deliberate control of ascent rate at a crucial depth. Account should be taken of the increased dive time when arriving at an appropriate surfacing code for the dive.

Traditional tables have encouraged a blinkered thought process in considering dive planning, in the stark contrast they have shown to 'no-stop' and 'decompression-stop' dives. Many divers have believed there is some inherent protection by sticking to no-stop dives. Reality is not like that – the situation is many shades of grey. The fact is that a no-stop dive to the limit can be more DCI-provocative than a dive just beyond the limit with an in-water stop.

Much of the reluctance to perform in-water stops has been based on the difficulties of actually doing them in North Atlantic waters. Many divers have now proved that such stops are perfectly feasible. This should not be read as an encouragement to race to the hairier extremes of the table, but rather to learn a technique which can make ascents safer.

There is no doubt that a direct ascent to the surface from many dives can encourage bubble formation. It is quite possible that this may be the cause of a number of DCI cases reported by divers following no-stop table profiles but appearing to have otherwise faithfully followed the table procedure. Another possible factor in many otherwise inexplicable DCI incidents where good dive practice has been followed is the existence of a PFO. The incidence of Patent Foramen Ovale (a sub-clinical hole in the heart) in the population could be as high as 25 per cent or even 30 per cent. It is currently impracticable to screen for a PFO with a diving medical, but the ability of bubbles to shunt from the venous to the arterial blood within the heart provides a ready mechanism for DCI. In such situations careful non-bubble-provocative ascent techniques are very desirable and many believe slow ascent procedures play an important role in reducing the rate of bubble formation as the body tissues out-gas. Although the decompression process is not complete, the surface is where the dive stops – when approaching a red traffic light it is better to be slowing down than accelerating! Awareness and control of ascent rate should be an important feature of every dive.

Nitrogen narcosis

Between 20 and 40m some narcotic effect is detectable in many divers

Between 40 and 50m reaction time and decision making is significantly impaired

Over 50m divers suffer serious narcotic impairment

Nitrogen narcosis

Nitrogen is normally regarded as an inert gas but we have already seen that its presence in the compressed air breathed by divers can cause decompression problems if not properly taken into account. Sadly, this is not the end of the nitrogen story. While having no apparent effect on our bodies at normal atmospheric pressures, this is not the case when the ambient pressure increases. We need to recall that in a mixture of gases as the pressure increases, so the partial pressure of each constituent gas increases in proportion to its presence in the mixture. It appears that as the partial pressure of nitrogen in the body tissues increases, it starts to exert a narcotic effect on the nervous system. While a clear understanding of the process has yet to transpire, it would seem that under increased pressure the nitrogen interferes with the normal passage of signals in the nervous system. While the process may not be fully understood, the effects are well documented. Different divers vary in their precise response and the depths at which symptoms occur. The nature and onset depth of symptoms may even vary for a particular diver from dive to dive – but symptoms there are!

Essentially, the effects can be likened to those caused by alcohol consumption, with increasing depth being similar to increasing consumption. Breathing nitrogen at ever greater partial pressure reduces the ability of the diver to think and reason effectively. This is often manifested by a difficulty to interpret a contents gauge, a watch or a dive computer reading. By concentrating hard this effect can usually be overcome, but should be taken as a warning sign. In the extreme the diver will become unconscious, which underwater is usually going to result in death. Fortunately, the narcotic effect is gradual and if the process is understood ample warning symptoms are apparent to avoid such extremes. Most divers using compressed air experience narcotic performance impairment even before 30m but are unaware of this degradation. At 40m most divers do become aware of significant narcotic effect and most consider 50m a sensible limit for compressed-air diving. Other breathing-gas mixtures with reduced nitrogen content help decrease narcosis problems for deeper dives.

Similar to the effects of excess alcohol consumption, the slowing of thought processes and reactions are usually accompanied by emotional or mood changes. Again as with alcohol, these changes affect different divers in different ways. Some experience a carefree feeling of euphoria while others describe feelings of anxiety and apprehension. As depth increases, so these feelings seem to intensify, even to the extent of producing a state of panic. Divers describe an increased awareness of their heartbeat and respiration, along with sensations such as 'hearing' a pulse and narrowing of vision.

Fortunately for diving, the remedy is very simple – reduce the ambient pressure by ascending. This has a further advantage over drink-related problems – there is no hangover and relief of symptoms is immediate. In practical terms, divers need to be conscious of the slowing of responses with depth and be aware of the effects of nitrogen narcosis on both themselves and their buddies. Dive plans should always bear this in mind. If the effects become at all threatening to the conduct of the dive, divers should ascend immediately to a shallow enough depth that the symptoms are no longer a problem. Ignoring the effects of nitrogen narcosis can have grave consequences, the so-called 'rapture of the deep' has claimed the lives of divers who have ignored its consequences.

It is worth remembering that while the degree and onset of narcosis you might experience may well vary from dive to dive, there are possible pre-disposing factors. Anxiety, fatigue and poor physical condition seem connected to shallower onset and increased severity of symptoms, so all are conditions it is sensible to avoid or minimise before diving. The prior consumption of alcohol or other drugs which have a similar effect on the nervous system also appear to combine with any high-pressure nitrogen effect to amplify any narcotic symptoms, so don't drink and dive!

Don't drink and dive

Carbon dioxide toxicity

The metabolic process uses oxygen and blood sugars to produce energy and in the process also produces carbon dioxide. This carbon dioxide is normally exhaled into the atmosphere and, other than contributing to global warming, does not adversely affect us. The exhalation process is not total, as a small amount of expired air remains in our breathing passages, that is the nose, mouth, throat and lungs. Therefore, our inhalations contain a slightly higher proportion of carbon dioxide than exists in the atmosphere surrounding us. This internal body volume still left with exhaled air is referred to as 'dead' space. As soon as we breathe through external equipment such as a snorkel or a regulator, this dead space will be increased and the proportion of carbon dioxide in the inhalation also increased. As long as the dead space is not too great this is not a problem, but should the inhaled carbon dioxide level become too large, major difficulties can be encountered.

Effectively, the cause of the build-up of carbon dioxide in the blood is inadequate ventilation, which can result from shallow breathing and over-exertion. As a result the diver may experience nausea, vomiting, dizziness, headache, flushing, panting or shortness of breath. Extreme cases can produce confusion, convulsions and loss of consciousness, all potentially very serious. With properly functioning equipment and uncontaminated breathing-gas supplies, divers who breathe normally and avoid over exertion are unlikely to experience difficulties in this area.

Carbon monoxide toxicity

Carbon monoxide toxicity

Not usually present in the atmosphere to any harmful extent, carbon monoxide should not normally be a diving hazard. However, it is a by-product of running internal combustion engines and sometimes such engines are used to power diving compressors. Should the compressor air inlet be positioned too close to the engine's exhaust, or to other sources such as passing traffic or boat engines, the compressed breathing gas can be contaminated with carbon monoxide. As many compressors are oil-lubricated, wear and faulty maintenance can also create carbon monoxide internally, which can contaminate air that was clean at the inlet. When inhaled, carbon monoxide is readily absorbed by the blood and is taken up by the haemoglobin in preference to its normal cargo – our life-giving oxygen – by a factor of around 200 times! As a result, the supply of oxygen to the body is reduced with potentially very serious results. There are no real warnings because carbon monoxide is both colourless and odourless, symptoms are those of hypoxia (reduced blood oxygen levels), namely headaches, confusion and unconsciousness.

Fortunately this form of contamination is extremely rare, but it is well worth challenging breathing-gas supplies that taste oily or otherwise contaminated. It is also very relevant that smoking tobacco also produces carbon monoxide and a typical smoker's blood has about five to ten per cent of the blood's oxygen-carrying capability knocked out by this poisonous gas, making the diver hypoxic before he or she even starts the dive. Smoking is never a good idea, but is especially to be avoided before and after diving when respiratory efficiency is at a premium.

Oxygen toxicity

Oxygen is an essential gas for our living processes and is breathed by the diver as a component of compressed air. However, oxygen can create serious, even fatal, consequences for the diver if used incorrectly. Within the normal recreational diving range, breathing compressed air should not expose the diver to any real oxygen problems. Difficulties only arise should we go beyond this normal range to depths where the partial pressure of oxygen is significantly elevated.

So how does this indispensable gas come to be a threat to divers?

Pulmonary toxicity

Breathing raised levels of oxygen has long been used medicinally, particularly in situations such as lung damage where the body's ability to absorb oxygen from atmospheric air is diminished. Studies on such usage have shown that long-term respiratory exposure to high levels of oxygen causes damage to the lungs, which if maintained could be fatal. Breathing 60-per-cent oxygen for just 12 hours can cause pulmonary toxic damage and irritation, producing swelling of the alveolar walls causing symptoms such as wheezing, coughing and shortness of breath. This, of course, is at surface pressure, where the oxygen is being breathed at a pressure of 0.6 bar. To reproduce these conditions in diving you would need to breathe compressed air at a depth of 20m, where the respiratory gas pressure would be 3 bar, so giving an oxygen partial pressure of (3 x 0.2) 0.6 bar. Quite feasible in terms of depth, but not usually for 12-hour time periods. It is believed that the increased level of oxygen damages the surfactant coating of the cells lining the lungs. Over the relatively short exposure periods and concentrations experienced by air-breathing divers this form of oxygen toxicity is unlikely to be a problem. The surfactant is regenerated following exposures of only a few hours. However, this is of relevance to divers breathing other gas mixtures with elevated oxygen percentages, as discussed later.

CNS toxicity

Of more immediate consequence is a second form of oxygen poisoning, one which involves the central nervous system (CNS). Some experts believe that CNS toxicity problems may start to arise when a diver is breathing oxygen at partial pressures from 0.9 bar upwards, and most training organisations advise limiting respiratory oxygen partial pressures to between 1.4 and 1.6 bar. The exact cause of CNS toxicity has yet to be proved, but may well involve the high oxygen levels generating an excessive production of free radicals such as hydrogen peroxide. This radical has been shown to trigger sporadic 'firing' of nerve synapses so may well be involved in the CNS toxicity process. While not a desirable state of affairs, in itself CNS poisoning does not usually pose a life-threatening situation. When they exist, early symptoms include lip tingling, visual disturbances, ringing in the ears, dizziness, anxiety, confusion and a lack of movement coordination. This continues on to

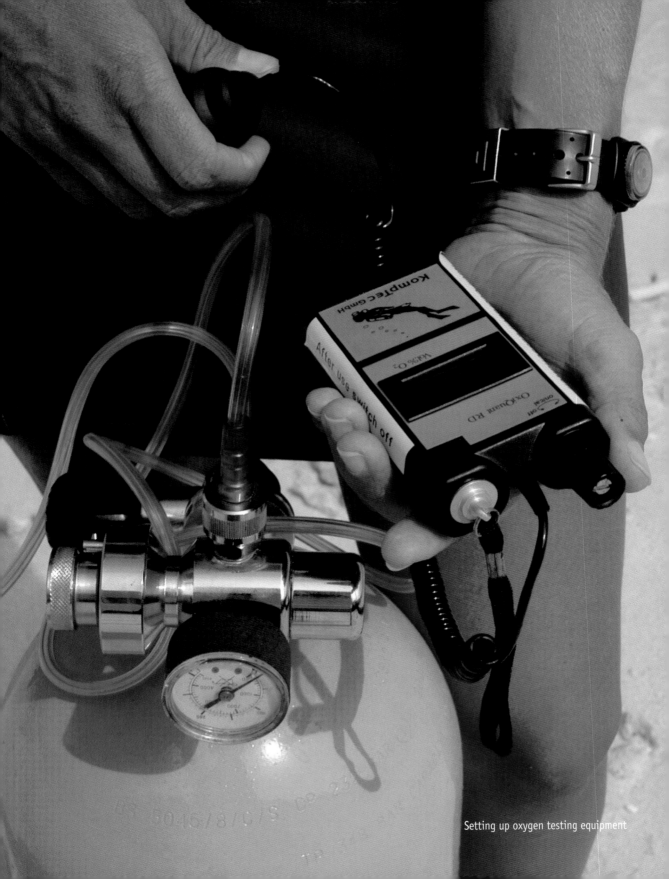

Setting up oxygen testing equipment

Gas mixes other than air

Using Nitrox

convulsions and finally cause the sufferer to fall into a coma. Occurring on land under medical supervision this is normally manageable, but underwater produces a dramatically more serious situation. A diver suffering convulsions or in a coma underwater is at very high risk from drowning. Making the situation even graver is that the early symptoms are often either not present or appear very transiently before a convulsion, making them useless as any kind of early warning guide. The treatment is a return to normal air breathing, but this may result in a short period when symptoms worsen, even to the extent of a short blackout.

All in all, CNS toxic events must be avoided when diving, so the subject needs to be well understood by all those potentially at risk. In the case of a diver breathing compressed air, performing a precise calculation assuming an oxygen content of 21 per cent, we see that an oxygen partial pressure of 1.4 bar will be reached when the ambient pressure is 6.67 bar (1.4 bar / 0.21), or a depth of 57m. Taking nitrogen narcosis into account, this is why many believe 50m is a sensible limiting depth for air-breathing recreational diving. Within the UK (and a number of other European countries) Health and Safety regulations limit air-breathing working divers to this depth range. The 1.4 bar limit is regarded as a safe limit for the vast majority of people, taking into account that different people exhibit different tolerances to hyperoxic exposure. Your tolerance may even vary from day to day or be affected by other factors such as raised levels of carbon dioxide or other substances in the body.

It is also believed that repetitive diving can produce an accumulative effect, so tables have been derived based on the principle of an oxygen 'dose'. The length and severity of exposure, based on time, concentration and pressure are used to calculate this dose and the diver can then ensure that successive dives produce a dose level within safe daily limits. Usually this is more of a concern for divers who are breathing gas mixtures other than air or using oxygen as a decompression enhancing gas.

Breathing gas mixes other than air

The limitations of air as a breathing gas for diving have long been recognised in the naval and commercial sectors. Today, as diving limits are ever pushed deeper and longer, mixtures commonly referred to as 'Trimix' are in regular use by some recreational divers. Even more common is the use of 'Nitrox', a term covering any mixture of nitrogen and oxygen where the percentage of oxygen is greater than that in air. The objective is to provide the diver with a respiratory gas mix which removes or reduces the toxic or narcotic effects or the decompression penalty experienced breathing air under pressure.

Nitrox

Examining Nitrox first, there are a number of factors which must be considered to enable such mixtures to be safely used by the diver. If we confine ourselves for the moment to a mixture in common usage in this area, Nitrox 32, a mixture of 32-per-cent oxygen and 68-per-cent nitrogen, we can immediately see the attraction of the reduction in nitrogen. The onset of narcosis is likely to be delayed and for any given dive parameters, the absorption of nitrogen reduced, so decreasing decompression penalties. In turn this can mean a diver breathing Nitrox32, yet following a decompression regime based on breathing air, will be decompressing for a higher level of tissue gas than exists, so producing a greater decompression safety margin. Alternatively, if a Nitrox32 decompression regime is followed, the time needed for decompression will be reduced compared to an equivalent dive performed using air.

Against this we need to offset the extra limitations imposed by Nitrox use. Firstly, the actual production is more complex. Because elevated oxygen percentages increase fire and explosion risks, if equipment comes into contact with pure oxygen or mixes with an oxygen content greater than air, it will need to be oxygen compatible and oxygen 'clean'. All materials must be compatible with such usage and there must be no trace of oil, grease or other hydrocarbons. For all gas mixtures other than air, procedures will need to be adopted to ensure that the mixture breathed by the diver is correct. Typically this involves measuring oxygen content on dive cylinder filling and again just before diving.

While using Nitrox lowers the narcosis barrier, in doing so it raises the oxygen toxicity barrier. By raising the percentage of oxygen in the breathing gas, toxic levels will occur at shallower depths. For example, with Nitrox32 the 1.4 bar level is reached at an ambient pressure of 4.375 bar (1.4 bar / 0.32), a depth of only 33m. It is important that any diver using such mixtures is always aware of this oxygen toxicity depth limit, calculating and recording in advance the Maximum Operating Depth (MOD) imposed by their particular mix. Tables are published to help discover MODs to avoid dangerous mathematical errors. As Nitrox use is frequently linked to extended dive times, the increased oxygen exposure also can lead to greater risk of pulmonary toxic damage. For this reason Nitrox divers must also track their oxygen 'dose', especially when repetitive diving within a day or on successive days.

Probably the most significant use of Nitrox is as a decompression gas, that is, a gas used to enhance or accelerate in-water decompression stops. This will normally entail the diver carrying a complete second diving cylinder and regulator which will only be

Preparing for a Nitrox dive

used during the in-water decompression stage of the dive. In this case the main breathing gas, often air, is commonly referred to as the 'bottom gas'. Breathing Nitrox during the stop means the lower levels of inhaled and therefore arterial nitrogen will speed up the diffusion of dissolved tissue nitrogen. Such use provides the diver with the choice of taking the benefit as an acceleration of the process by means of shorter in-water stop time, or merely as an added safety margin, following normal air-stop times.

The BSAC runs a number of Nitrox courses each year

Trimix

Trimix is an attempt to resolve the difficulties posed to air divers by deeper depths, the problems of both narcosis and oxygen toxicity. The obvious solution to reduce the narcotic effects posed by the nitrogen in breathing air is to reduce the proportion of nitrogen. A similar solution for oxygen toxicity is to reduce the proportion of oxygen. Then the first problem to be overcome is that if the relative proportions of both of these constituent gases are to be reduced, another gas has to be introduced to take up the missing proportion. It is important that this added, or diluent, gas is as inert as possible, introducing no new problems or harmful effects to the diver when breathed either at the surface or under pressure. A number of choices may be considered, generally from the family of inert gases, but hydrogen has been used experimentally for very some deep (500m) dives. Of the inert gases, xenon is narcotic and expensive, krypton causes dizziness, radon is radioactive, argon is also highly narcotic, really leaving only helium and neon as choices. Neon has been used successfully in a number of trials but remains expensive. This means helium tends to win as the least expensive, though certainly not cheap, solution.

So normal Trimix is a mixture of oxygen, nitrogen and helium, the actual proportions being varied to suit the dive target depth. A normoxic mix will have 21-per-cent oxygen, a hyperoxic mix more than 21-per-cent oxygen, and the most common used hypoxic mixes will have less than 21-per-cent oxygen for deeper dives. These mixtures are usually classified by the percentages of oxygen and helium, thus Trimix 17/60 is a mixture of 17-per-cent oxygen, 40-per-cent helium, the remaining 43 per cent being nitrogen. A breathing gas to be used at the surface must contain at least 16-per-cent oxygen to avoid any lack of oxygen or hypoxic problems. As helium demands a heavier decompression penalty than nitrogen, Trimix divers use Nitrox to enhance and accelerate the decompression schedule by switching to these gases at depths they can safely be used during the ascent from depth. So a Trimix diver may need two or even three separate breathing systems, Trimix for bottom use, Nitrox as a travelling gas for part of the ascent and a richer Nitrox as a final decompression gas in the shallower depths of decompression. The difficulty in deep Trimix diving is not mastering the theory behind it, or even the production of suitable breathing-gas mixtures – it is the sheer logistics of safely carrying and managing the various cylinders and regulators, each providing different life-support capability in their own depth zones. ☐

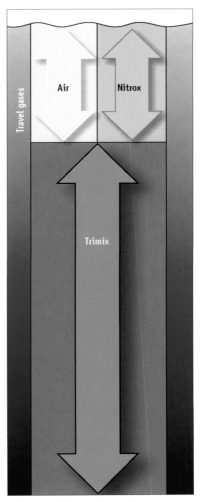

The use of Trimix allows for deeper dives

Chapter four
Diving the plan

You've planned your dive, so now it's time to dive your plan. When dive leading, you will bring to bear all the diving skills you have learned throughout your training. You will need to be aware of the divers you are leading, both their equipment and your own, and the different techniques required for specific types of diving.

Marshalling

Good dive marshals will convey their enthusiasm for diving to the divers they are marshalling

Dive marshalling

The dive marshal (DM) is the person with the ultimate responsibility for diving operations and so must also be accorded the ultimate decision-making power. Typically, the DM will remain at the surface supervising the diving activities, appointing a deputy to take over should they dive themselves. It is certainly not the job of the DM to do all the work, rather to delegate the simpler tasks and ensure they are performed adequately and timely. A major task

the DM would normally perform is that of pairing up divers and approving their dive plans. On large boats the DM would be the main communication channel between the captain and the divers during diving operations. In conjunction with the captain the DM will supervise the departure and recovery of divers. The overall briefing on the diving activities will normally be delivered by the DM.

An important job, often confused with marshalling,

A dive marshal assists a diver

When buddy diving verifying equipment operation prior to diving is important

is that of record keeping. While it is the job of the DM to ensure this happens, the record-keeping task is easy to delegate. Accurate records should be kept of the dive start and end times of all divers, of maximum depth attained, of dive pairings and any notable occurrences. Recording some equipment details such as cylinder size, start and end-pressure readings is useful, and if a breathing mix other than air is used the details must also be recorded. Various slates are available to help record such information, which should later be transcribed in a more permanent format.

The DM should ensure that emergency equipment such as a first-aid kit and therapeutic oxygen are available and in good order, and the contact details and a communication system with relevant emergency services are available. Should any incident arise, it should be the DM who controls the reaction. Decisions on the use of SMBs will rest with the DM, who should also supervise the setting-up of any decompression stations. No divers should enter the water until permitted by the DM, who must also make sure a lookout is kept for any possible endangerment to the divers by surface craft. This lookout can also signal the arrival of divers at stop depths, either by direct observation or spotting delayed SMBs, and the

arrival of divers at the surface. Observation of the dive site should be continuous – not just when divers are programmed to surface – as dives may be curtailed for many reasons, including emergencies.

Buddy-leading skills

Previous diving experience will have familiarised you with many aspects of buddy diving, the system whereby a pair of divers prepare and dive together, each looking after the other and prepared to offer assistance if needed. Naturally, during your early dives the caring element tends to be rather one-sided, with most responsibility borne first by your instructor and later by your dive leader. As your knowledge and skills develop you become a more active contributor to this mutual-assistance system. Now you are ready to take the role of dive leader and need to understand what extra responsibilities this will involve.

Dive planning has already been covered, so we can move on to the dive itself. Firstly, there will need to be a communication process, where as a dive leader you explain necessary details of the intended dive. This should not involve a blow-by-blow account of how you have researched and planned the dive, just

Buddy leading skills

Dive leaders and buddies preparing to enter the water

a condensed 'need to know' provision of information where a lot of words can often be avoided by using a simple sketch of the dive site. Sometimes this information may be provided in stages, such as general points on the projected dive and necessary equipment before leaving for the dive site, followed by more details on arrival at the site. Always bear in mind the difficulty of communicating in a boat while at sea, especially in a small RIB with space at a premium. Absorbing and retaining a lot of detail just before kitting up to dive is not feasible, so limit your communication to essential points.

Once aboard the dive boat it is useful to ensure your buddy's equipment is stowed near your own and that you can closely assist in their pre-dive preparation.

Keep an eye on your buddy during kitting up and be certain that you understand the operation of their equipment as well as your own. Following the pre-dive buddy check it is advisable that as the dive leader you enter the water first, to be immediately available to resolve any problems that might occur. Similarly, you should always be the deeper during the descent as then you are in a position to halt your buddy if any difficulties arise, for example, if one of your ears is slow to clear. Obviously you need to remain close and to be able to observe and assist your buddy at all times during the descent. Once on the bottom you will be acting as guide, so your buddy will follow your lead. Given your restricted field of vision underwater it is both sensible and more comfortable for your buddy

DIVE LEADER BRIEF

DIVE OBJECTIVE		
DIVE PLAN REVIEW	Entry ✓	
	Descent ✓	
	Dive ✓	
	Ascent ✓	
	Exit ✓	
	Problem response ✓	
SIGNALS	Standard ✓	
	Special ✓	
EQUIPMENT REVIEW	Standard ✓	
	Special ✓	
GAS AND EQUIPMENT CHECK		

A dive leader brief checklist

Equipment assembly

to swim by your side rather than behind you. Make sure you keep a close watch on time, depth, gas and direction. Make periodic checks on your buddy's gauges as well as your own – often this can be done discreetly, avoiding a 'mother hen' flavour to your dive-control technique. As dive leader you will be responsible for the use and control of extra equipment, such as an SMB or wreck reel (covered later).

When time for the ascent is reached you will communicate this to your buddy and operate the reverse of the descent procedure. You should now either be shallower than your buddy or closely positioned in order to control the ascent speed and direction. If appropriate, deploy your delayed SMB and control the depth and time of any in-water stops. On arrival at the surface, check your buddy is okay and signal to the surface party. Help your buddy with gear removal and water exit, remain in the water yourself until last so as to be in the best place to resolve problems. Once un-kitted, conduct a de-brief with your buddy and record details of the dive. As you share their pleasure you can bask in a glow of satisfaction as the person who made it happen!

Personal equipment and configuration

One of the most enjoyable sensations when diving is that feeling of freedom, and one of the most unwelcome is the opposite – entanglement. We are obliged to carry various equipment when diving, some essential for life support, some more task-oriented. How these items are carried is probably the most decisive factor in enjoying your freedom and avoiding snagging.

The aim is to achieve as much streamlining as possible, avoiding dangling hoses, gauges, straps and equipment that juts out and interferes with a smooth outline. This has the added advantage of creating your best possible hydrodynamic form, so reducing drag to a minimum and avoiding wasted effort when moving through the water. The first task in streamlining is to make sure everything is tailored to fit you. Take your mask straps – once these are adjusted to fit you, the excess strap lengths can be taped back against the head strap to keep the loose ends from flapping about. DIN screw regulator fittings are much less snag-prone than the A-clamp style. Many BCs have a whole range of straps which can flap and dangle, so once the BC is adjusted to your size, make sure as many of these straps as possible are taped or tucked out of the way.

A streamlined diver

Equipment such as knives should be stowed properly in sheaths

Pockets on BCs can be used to store various bits of equipment

Wing-style BCs are usually user-configured by adding equipment pouches using webbing attachments or D-ring clips. Make sure equipment does not dangle unnecessarily. Weight belt straps/weight harnesses tend to be 'one size fits all' so trim yours to be just right for you. Streamlining is important, but remember that underwater your mask will restrict your field of vision and your reach will be compromised by your diving gear. The next consideration is how the bits of equipment are stowed about you when you dive. There is not a great deal of flexibility with primary equipment such as your BC, main cylinder and regulator, pony cylinder and alternate regulator, but secondary equipment such as gauges, knife, torch, delayed SMB and reel can provide improvement and fine-tuning possibilities. The overriding principle is that such items must be easily found and put into operation, otherwise there is no point in carrying them. That said, the way in which you attach and stow them can make a big difference to your streamlined form and snag potential. While equipment manufacturers are sensitive to these issues, judicious use of thin bungee cord, rubber bands cut from cycle or other vehicle inner tubes and the ubiquitous surgical tubing can get you that much nearer to the ideal.

A good BC will have ample and accessible pockets, one where your delayed SMB and reel can be stowed and one where a small torch can be carried. Many of these pockets will have an adjacent lanyard attachment point. BC inflation hoses should be run together and not create untidy loops, the same applying to octopus regulators, with quick-release stowage in an obvious position that does not leave loops of hose dangling beside you. Probably the worst entanglement culprits are enormous gauge consoles – if you must have one, make sure it does not create a hazard for you. Many divers run the hose under the arm, tucking it inside the BC so the console or gauge just protrudes at waist level. If you adopt this technique, make sure it does not leave a loop of hose behind you and that you can easily read the gauge when needed.

You must always be able to locate and operate the equipment you carry!

Boat diving

Space is valuable when kitting up

Efficient kitting-up skills are even more important in the confines of a RIB

Boat diving

While dive leading is rightly thought of as an underwater activity, there is frequently a surface transport element involved. This may be a simple commercial arrangement such as booking onto a day dive cruise boat or it could range from organising a group charter of a liveaboard to being in charge of a diving club's RIB.

Details of expedition planning belong in another volume, but as a dive leader you can expect to play a more significant role in these activities than as a novice diver. Take every opportunity to increase your knowledge and skills in boat handling and navigation. Remember, at sea ultimate responsibility lies with the captain, and hence so does ultimate power. The captain's word, literally, is law. Observe how the boat is operated, gain an understanding of why things are done in a particular manner. If you are more aware of what is happening and why it is happening in that way, you will better appreciate the normal running of the boat and how to behave appropriately and helpfully. Thus you will be less likely to get in the way, making life more pleasant for both yourself and the divers who you are guiding.

Diving from various types of vessels has been covered in the first volume of *The Diving Manual*, but as a dive leader you will normally be responsible to the dive controller or marshal for the organisation of yourself and your buddy. Before the dive, this is guided by the requirements of the dive, but you will still have responsibilities after the dive. Ensure that the dive details are properly recorded, especially information that will have an impact on a subsequent dive such as decompression requirements. Remember that you will both still be decompressing for quite some time after a dive. It is sensible to avoid demanding physical activity immediately after the dive, and this should include avoiding pulling up a heavy anchor or shot-line or strenuous swimming. Snorkel diving will modify the decompression process and could even create a 'yo-yo' diving risk if micro-bubbles are still present. So, once the gear is stowed away you have a good excuse to relax and replay the dive with your buddy.

Boats provide access to a wide variety of dive sites

A diver checks his computer while decompressing

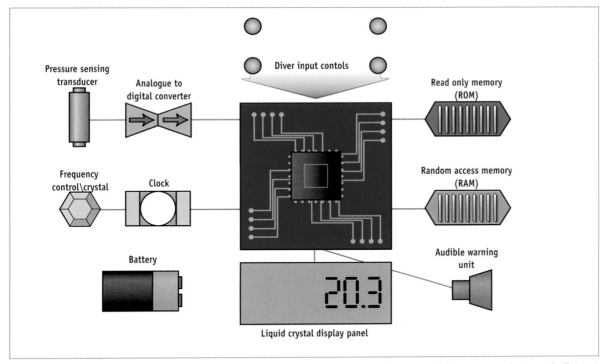

Pressure sensing transducer

Analogue to digital converter

Diver input contols

Read only memory (ROM)

Frequency control\crystal

Clock

Random access memory (RAM)

Battery

Audible warning unit

20.3

Liquid crystal display panel

Besides sensing water pressure, most dive computers will also sense changes in atmospheric pressure and automatically start the device on sensing the increased pressure upon immersion. Some models may also sense breathing-gas pressure. The ROM contains the computer's programme and uses an algorithm to process elapsed time and pressure changes in order to calculate decompression requirements. The RAM is used to store measurements and calculation results both during and after the dive, though all of this data is normally not permanently available. The LCD panel and audible-warning unit pass information to the diver. Some displays have a backlight option, useful in low-visibility and night-dive situations.

Diving with computers

A device that would automatically calculate levels of gas absorbed by a diver and then provide information that would allow a safe release of that gas has long been seen as desirable. Specifications for such a device existed in the early 1950s, but the first commercially successful devices did not appear until the early 1980s when suitable transducers, microprocessor, memory chips, liquid-crystal displays and batteries became available. In 1983 the Decobrain 1 and the Edge computers came on the market and the age of computer diving really commenced. These devices were improved and then a second generation of smaller devices such as the Suunto, Aladin and Skinny Dipper were produced at lower prices than the first-generation machines.

As more knowledge and experience in using dive computers has become available, so designs have been further improved, newer devices exhibiting extra features, improved displays and much longer battery life. The ability for a computer to actually sense tissue gas loads is not currently feasible, the best that can be done is tracking the pressure exposure of the diver and then calculating the gas load in real time.

A major impact of dive computers is that they make it far easier to monitor 'multi-level' dives. The computer assumes that steps within the ruling rectangular dive profile result in lower tissue gas loads and can thus produce an extension to the allowed dive time. It is obvious that decompression tables and ascents with staged decompression stops describe only a small section of possible dive profiles. Dive computers, which compute various tissue gas loads as the dive progresses and continuously calculate decompression requirements from these values, can more accurately

Computers

A typical dive computer display showing the diver at a depth of 15.8m with an elapsed time of 50 minutes

register atmospheric pressure before commencing a dive. Best are the devices that can be automatically switched into dive mode by detecting a pressure change. Such an initiation is relatively diver-proof.

The next essential element is a suitably accurate pressure transducer unaffected by temperature changes in typical diving environments. This can be used to provide the diver with information about both current and historically attained depths, including the maximum depth achieved. Pressure readings, coupled with time measurement, are used by the computer to calculate other information for display to the diver. Remaining no-stop time, decompression stop time and depth and total time required for the ascent are other desirable information displays. Some computers refer to the depth of the deepest required decompression stop as the 'ceiling' above which the diver cannot ascend until the stop is complete. Along with the improvements in algorithm processing speed, pressure-sampling rates have increased and better indications are being provided together with ascent-rate audible warnings showing when set fixed critical rates are being exceeded.

Some computers have a second pressure transducer, which measures and displays air-cylinder pressure. A number of these devices are console-mounted, attached to the dive regulator via a high-pressure hose. Some of these are not easily detachable and hence less portable. Others employ a sensor mounted directly on a high-pressure port on the regulator first stage, which transmits by radio signal to a wrist-mounted dive computer unit. The air-pressure values obtained can be used by the algorithm, in conjunction with the clock data, to calculate current air consumption and thus provide an estimated dive duration display. Ambient temperature is also measured and displayed by a number of computers.

Before the dive most computers will sense current atmospheric pressure, some displaying this directly, others using it as an altitude correction factor and displaying this symbolically. Many will also scroll through a number of predicted rectangular profile dives giving no-stop times against a range of depths. An extension of this capability is to allow the user to input particular dive parameters and obtain decompression planning information in advance of the dive. Other useful indications are a self-diagnostic test, often coupled with a check of all display elements and a battery-state warning.

simulate the tissue state and decompression needs of the diver. Such devices are often referred to as 'variable profile' or 'multi-level' computers. Using elapsed time and ambient pressure as inputs, calculations are repeatedly performed to update a set of simulated tissue gas-loading values. From these values, the most critical at any stage of the dive can be used to predict a decompression schedule.

The method followed to achieve these calculations is often referred to as an algorithm and it is the appropriateness of this algorithm which is important to the diver. Comparisons with conventional dive tables are only possible where rectangular dive profiles and the exact descent and ascent rates of that table are followed. Repetitive dive schedules are even more difficult to compare because computers are so precise in their measurement of dive parameters, whereas tables suffer from gross rounding-up effects which are accumulative.

An essential part of all dive computers is an accurate clock. Coupling this with either a manual or automatic switch means it can measure elapsed time during a dive and surface interval after the dive. Some models relied on a 'wet contact' system to start the computer running, but again problems could arise if it failed to

Computers in practice

Having earlier examined the theory of how dive computers work, it is worth considering the practical implications of their use. Many diving authorities had a very negative approach to the introduction of these devices, to a certain extent reacting against a perceived increase in decompression incidents. Although much of this perception proved unfounded, there was and still is a tendency among a small number of divers to erroneously believe that they can hand over thought processes about decompression to the computer. The computer provides the recreational diver with the most accurate depth monitoring we have ever enjoyed, a dramatic improvement on the earlier temperature-sensitive mechanical depth gauges. With the computer we benefit from precise time measurements which contrast well with the difficulty of reading a dive time on a watch bezel to better than +/− two minutes' accuracy. The danger with computer use is that they do their job so well the wearer may be tempted to forget the computer's job is just to advise and not to control the diver. While it is highly desirable that all divers use a computer, wearing one must not be taken as an excuse to skimp on personal knowledge, dive planning or self responsibility.

When diving in buddy pairs it is strongly advisable that both divers carry their own computer. Firstly, even on the same dive there can be slight differences in profile between buddies that cumulatively can produce different decompression demands, in which case the more conservative schedule must be followed by both. Secondly, the buddy pair may well follow different sequential dive patterns. They may have been diving with different buddies, in which case the one without a computer may well have no means of sorting out decompression requirements. In pairing divers who have previously dived, it makes sense wherever possible to pair people with similar decompression 'loadings' as they are then likely to have much the same decompression requirements.

For the travelling diver, owning your own dive computer can have advantages over hiring one at your destination, an important advantage is that your computer can travel with you. This means it experiences the same ambient-pressure changes during the journey that you do and, provided it has a sufficiently sophisticated algorithm, can better simulate subsequent dives. As a wrist-mounted computer is easier to carry (or even wear) on an aircraft, this may also be considered a point of preference over console-mounted models.

The purpose of the computer is to accurately measure dive parameters affecting your decompression requirements and to provide you with advice based on these measurements. In most cases it would be foolish to disregard this advice, but slavish adherence is also not always the most appropriate action. Just because the computer is advising a stop at 3m does not mean that is the sole option. Frequently a deeper stop, at, say, 6m, will be more comfortable and easier to accurately maintain. Physiologically this is acceptable and a good computer will happily accept your variation of its projected profile, informing you when it considers it safe to proceed to the surface, the 3m stop omitted. While normally extremely reliable, it is certainly not impossible for a computer to fail while in use, especially when its battery level is low. Take careful note of any battery-state information it provides, and replace it sooner rather than later, especially prior to an extended diving trip.

Computer failure during a dive may be sudden or progressive. A few models will display time and depth only for a short time, conserving battery power, while others will either display nothing or give extremely improbable readings. Whichever, it is vital that you have a bail-out plan. The simplest is to follow your buddy's computer, possibly adding or extending any decompression stops. This action, of course, relies on you both having similar diving histories during your current dive sequence. If there is any doubt, the dive should be terminated immediately but you still need to have a safe surfacing procedure, something a good dive plan will have provided for. It is a good idea to always carry a small plastic slate with alternative surfacing solutions for the dive you are performing should the exact plan not be followed.

A selection of modern dive computers

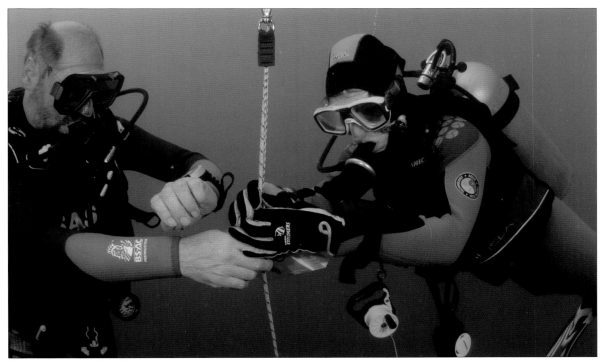

Divers checking their dive time and decompression requirements during the ascent

Dive data recording

Another consequence of the digital revolution is that computers – like George Washington – never lie. Your dive profile has been recorded and can be checked by others! Following the dive, key values are reported, which are useful to both the diver and the dive marshal, and form the basis for recording the dive in personal and group dive logs. Some computers retain a record of sampled time/depth readings, enabling a dive profile to be produced, and may also record events such as an ascent-speed violation. Dive computers that also interface with a personal computer allow detailed profile graphs to be printed and electronic dive logs to be kept.

Decompression diving

Undertaking any dive that requires a compulsory in-water decompression stop is undoubtedly a serious undertaking. If an in-water decompression stop must

be made, it creates a barrier between the diver and a safe ascent to the surface, similar in some respects to a no-clear-surface dive. The fact that this barrier is not physical does not make it any less dangerous, indeed it can make it more difficult to monitor correctly. For any dive needing planned decompression stops rather than just precautionary stops, it is wise to first ask the question – why are you doing it? As a risk-increasing factor, you need good reason to justify such dives and must take all possible steps to minimise the increased risk. Increased depth/time exposures should not be done just for their own sake, particularly if the driving force is 'rapture of the depth gauge', simply the desire to log greater depths. Shallower depths usually provide more light and life, where warmer, longer and often more interesting dives may be carried out.

Assuming this has all been duly taken into consideration and there is a justifiable reason for the dive, the next step is to consider the preparation of

Decompression diving

Ascending to a decompression stop

the participating divers. It is worth mentioning here that such diving is not advisable for some individuals, particularly anyone diagnosed as having a PFO. Usually the only reason anyone would know they have a PFO would be if they had previously suffered DCI, in this case probably performing a dive that would not demand in-water decompression stops. Having recognised the increased risk factor inherent in decompression-stop dives, there are a number of steps which can be taken to minimise and control this risk. Careful dive planning with regard to breathing-gas consumption is certainly called for. The inability of the diver to return directly to the surface is further compounded by the necessity to stop and maintain position at fixed, shallow depths on the ascent. The various skills needed to perform this technique must be learned and practised on dives when such stops are not needed, in case depth maintenance is not 100-per-cent successful. Only when all the divers concerned have shown an ability to perform such stops accurately

should real decompression stops be attempted.

The ability to maintain a constant depth is a major requirement, and in turn this demands total buoyancy control even when shallow. Don't forget that a large portion of breathing gas will already have been consumed during a dive needing stops and that this will have an effect on the diver's buoyancy, so these conditions should also apply when learning the technique. While the diver must be capable of neutral buoyancy at the stop depth, the most comfortable stops are often achieved with slightly negative buoyancy. A shot-line or some similar aid to hold on to makes this easier to attain and it should be emphasised that very little negative buoyancy is required. Finning either up or down to maintain stop depth is a sign of either too much negative or positive buoyancy. Besides making depth control very difficult, this action in itself may be more provocative in forming micro-bubbles and compromise the effectiveness of the stop.

The closer the stop is to the surface, the greater

the relative changes in pressure for any given vertical movement. This means that greater depth-keeping accuracy is demanded in a zone where any air volumes will undergo more rapid changes, in turn producing more rapid buoyancy fluctuations. Another factor making shallow decompression stops difficult to perform will be any wave action, where the influence is greater near the surface. The BSAC '88 tables employ a shallowest stop of 6m, rather than the more traditional final 3m stop, as this enables stops to be more accurately conducted, with considerably less stress on the diver. Despite the fact that some computers indicate a final stop depth or 'ceiling' of 3m, the computer algorithm should be able to cope if final stops are performed at 6m. The displayed time for the 3m stop may even clear more rapidly than initially displayed, as performing deeper stops can allow an earlier return to the surface because the ascent has been less provocative in micro-bubble formation.

Widely regarded as one of the most comfortable ways of performing in-water decompression stops, an underwater trapeze bar, or bars, is not too difficult to set up and deploy. The trapeze is set up to hang at the decompression depth, say 6m, possibly suspended directly from the dive boat, or maybe from independent buoys. If buoys are used they will need to be of fairly large buoyancy, typically at least 50kg, and greater if more than one bar is set up to allow stops at deeper depths, and a minimum of 10–15kg weight will be needed. The length of the bar should be chosen to suit the number of divers expected to be using it simultaneously, around 0.5m per diver works well. Select a bar diameter that is easy and comfortable to grip, scaffold pole is popular because it is also relatively heavy. Of course, it is useful if the metal is protected from rusting by being galvanised but it is difficult to protect the inside of the tube. Should lightweight stainless steel, aluminium or other material be used, the bar will probably need extra weighting to help stability when a number of divers are using it. Whenever any communal decompression aid is used, an extra-careful watch on depth must be maintained, as communal buoyancy or depth control may influence the actual depth of the aid. In particular, when new groups first arrive at the stop there is often a period of time needed for the overall buoyancy of the group to stabilise.

Once in-water stops are a necessary part of a dive, it becomes very important that the divers can locate the decompression station. Usually this is achieved by fol-

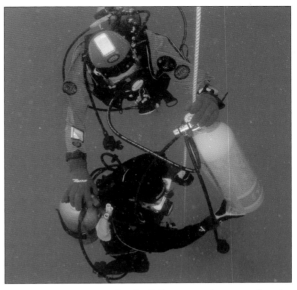

A pair of divers on a decompression stop

lowing a line such as an anchor or shot-line, possibly with a further travel line to guide the ascending divers across to the decompression station.

Providing the dive plan can ensure all groups have returned to the decompression station, it is also possible for quite complex decompression aids to be free-floating. That is to say that in circumstances where lengthy in-water stops are to be carried out, a structure such as a trapeze allowed to drift with the current can make such stops much more comfortable. As buoyancy control is easier, so safety will be increased, as long as surface cover can follow the drifting decompressing divers. Of course, it is important that all divers have arrived at the decompression station before it is set free to drift. Careful planning and aids such as a signing down and up list on a slate attached to the shot-line can help confirm everyone is accounted for. Buddy pairs may also adopt free-drifting decompression stops, often employing personal delayed surface marker buoys. It is essential that such procedures are planned and agreed in advance with the surface cover and that there is sufficient surface cover provision for the number of groups simultaneously decompressing.

The technique of inflating and using the delayed

An emergency breathing-gas supply at decompression depth

Lines organised for in-water stops

Divers decompressing on a trapeze

surface marker buoy (DSMB) must also be mastered. These buoys generally consist of a high visibility airtight material formed into a long (1–1.5m) tube of about 10cm diameter, completely sealed at one end. The other end often has a narrowed neck formed to reduce air spillage, though this also means inflation times are increased. Inflation is normally performed using an octopus supply and is something that requires practice to achieve a good standard of proficiency. The problem is that as soon as DSMB inflation starts, as you are holding on to it you will gain buoyancy and start to ascend, a process that can rapidly become uncontrollable as any residual buoyancy from your BC or drysuit will also increase. This means the DSMB must be inflated and released as quickly as possible, with personal buoyancy being reduced by a simultaneous full exhalation.

There is no need to completely inflate the DSMB as the reduction in pressure it experiences as it rises to the surface will compensate. Typically, if the inflation is conducted at around a depth of 9m, 50–60 per cent inflation is adequate. Of course, it is important to keep hold of the end of the attachment line when the DSMB is released! Maintain tension on the DSMB line at all times, as this will keep it upright at the surface, increasing visibility, keeping the open neck underwater and so stopping the air escaping. Sophisticated designs incorporate an automatic sealing mechanism that allows easy inflation but seals when the air expands to fill the DSMB. Such models also require over-pressure valves to prevent them bursting if they are over-filled. Even more sophisticated are those DSMBs that have integral inflation systems from a small, rechargeable air cylinder.

The attachment line is normally around 3mm in diameter and may be of about 10m in length simply stuffed into the DSMB before it is rolled up and stored in a BC pocket until needed. Another technique is to roll up the DSMB and then wind the attachment line around it before stowage. To help avoid entanglement when the line is freed, a small weight (200–500g) is often fastened to the free end. The simplest and preferred method is to accommodate the line on a small reel, allowing just the right amount of line to be deployed. Additionally, once stable at the stop depth, the reel may be clipped to the diver, a process many divers find makes the stop more comfortable.

An alternative method of performing stops in a

Decompression diving

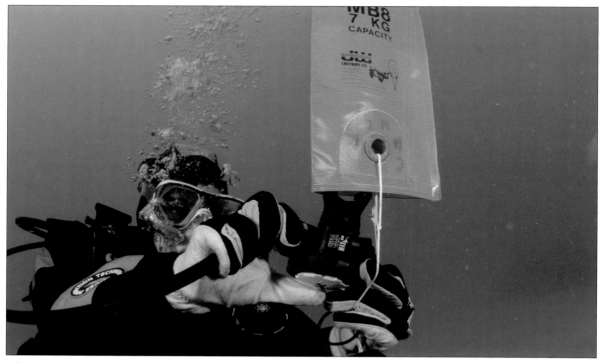

Inflating a delayed SMB

current – if drifting is not feasible – is for divers to attach themselves to the decompression station. Of course, attaching yourself to anything underwater is not something to be undertaken lightly, and for such stops this is usually achieved by means of a 'jon' line, a short line with quick-release clips, so that divers can quickly and simply release themselves. Ensure that the decompression station allows suitable attachment points for the numbers of divers likely to be present at any one time. The positioning should allow adequate separation and not cause all the divers to be swept together by the current into an uncomfortable bunch, which means effectively that each diver needs their own attachment point. An advantage of jon line use is that the diver is more isolated from wave-action depth changes of the decompression station.

Suspending one or more reserve breathing-gas cylinders, usually fitted with two second-stage regulators and long hoses, is also common practice. This is to provide extra security and should not remove or reduce

the need for advance air-requirement calculations and the need for divers to carry sufficient breathing gas to safely conduct the dive. The dive should always be capable of a successful conclusion with the gas carried by the diver, even if the planned decompression station cannot be located and the stop has to be conducted independently using a delayed SMB. If there are multiple stop depths planned for the decompression station, emergency cylinders are positioned in preference at the later, shallower stop levels, as this is where they are more likely to be needed. Some divers prefer to change breathing gas during decompression stops or at some other point in the ascent, typically to accelerate the decompression process. For some advanced dives, breathing gas may also be supplied from reserves on the surface by means of an umbilical and regulator second stages.

Multilevel diving

There is a particular style of diving that has long been practised when diving coral reefs or similar sites where the areas of interest extend from deep water almost to the surface. It involves starting the dive deep and gradually ascending, the latter part of the dive being of long duration in shallow water and equating to a decompression stop. The problem is that no decompression tables have been produced to describe this shape of profile, and if conventional rectangular profiles are used they are very punitive. Divers following such profiles are attempting to match their gradual ascent to the decompression needs of their tissues, but in doing so they are, of course, writing and proving (or disproving!) a new decompression schedule. While there is merit in this logic, in the past it has been difficult to support such profiles when the penalties for error are so severe. However, there are now methods to properly perform such diving. The simplest is the dive computer, which by continuously monitoring depth and calculating gas levels, automatically caters for such a profile.

The second is a technique to apply multi-level solutions to a decompression table to cater for an ascent in staged levels. To use this technique the dive *must* be planned in advance and divided into a sequence of ascending stages, each being treated as a separate dive. Effectively, you are assumed to surface from each stage and gain the appropriate surfacing code, but of course you just ascend to the next stage depth. The dive time of the first stage is from leaving the surface up to arrival at the next stage depth, successive stage dive times being measured from arrival at that stage to arrival at the next. Decompression requirements and appropriate surfacing codes for subsequent stages in the ascent are obtained by using the table indicated from the previous stage 'surfacing code'. The final stage dive time will terminate at 6m, from where, following any appropriate decompression, a normal ascent to the surface is made. Although there is an implied safety margin in this strategy because the ascents between each stage are imaginary, conducting multi-level dives within a single rectangular profile envelope will give an even greater safety margin.

Divers on a wall slowly ascend to the surface

Underwater navigation

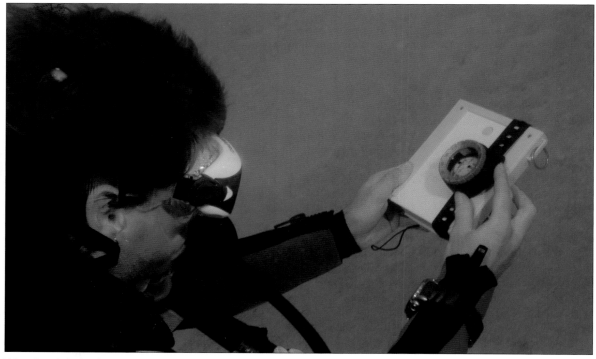

Using the edge of a slate as an extended sighting aid while navigating with a compass

Underwater navigation

Contrary to he belief of many divers, navigating underwater is not a mysterious black art and neither is the symbolic carrying of a compass a lucky charm to prevent the wearer becoming lost. Navigating underwater is really no more complex than navigating on the surface – the basic principles are the same and as with most skills it is practice and experience that ensures success. Just as on the surface, underwater you find your way around by recognising objects and forming a mental picture of their spatial relationship with one another. And just as when in a new place on the surface, it takes careful observation and time before you become familiar with a particular environment. Some divers see a dive as a route march and try to cover as much ground as possible in the time available. To hone your navigational skills it is far better to get to know a smaller area well, which will give you more time to observe your surroundings.

Many dives require that you find your way back to the start point and if that is the case, try to pick out prominent features on the outward leg of the dive. Obviously it helps if these features are within easy sight of each other and are just as prominent and recognisable when approached from the opposite direction. Besides having a mental picture of these objects you also need some idea of the relative distances separating them. For most people, distance estimation is not easy on land, and is even more difficult underwater. A useful tip is to judge distances against the length of your buddy (probably around 2m from head to fin tip). Counting fin strokes is fine in theory but rarely used in practice except in navigation exercises – timing the outward leg is generally much more practical in normal diving. To reinforce these skills after the dive, try to produce a sketch map of the route you have followed and listen to your dive buddy's comments on it, discussing the key points of the route will help cement your mental picture.

An understanding of how to use a compass is an essential skill

Underwater navigation

A compass mounted on a console with contents gauge

This form of navigation is known as pilotage.

Having so rudely dismissed the magnetic compass earlier, we had better resurrect it, as it does have a very important role to play. It is important to realise that if you do not understand how to use a compass on dry land you are unlikely to be successful underwater. Providing it is not affected by nearby magnetic material or other magnetic fields, a compass needle will come to rest lined up with the Earth's magnetic north and south poles. Knowing the direction of magnetic north, any other direction can then be deduced. Note that a compass will not give a correct reading if the needle is unable to swing freely. This can occur if it is tilted too far out of the horizontal.

The simplest use of the compass is to use it to measure the direction you take on the outward leg of the dive and then, by adding or subtracting 180 to this direction, obtain a reciprocal bearing to indicate the return direction. Used in conjunction with pilotage this can provide quite effective navigation. If you need to navigate across areas with few useful pilotage features, you should set your direction-of -travel bearing on your compass and align the needle with magnetic north. Holding the compass steady on this setting, sight as distant an object you can see in line with the compass direction-of-travel indicator and swim to that object. Once there you can repeat the process until your destination is reached. To help the sighting process and to record bearings, some divers fasten their compass to a plastic slate, using the edge of the slate as an extended sighting aid. To properly navigate underwater (and to enjoy the dive) you need to be fully aware of your surroundings. The 'joining the dots' method of compass use is more practical and agreeable than swimming along with your eyes glued to your compass trying to keep the needle in the 'gate.'

In extreme conditions compounded by low visibility, it may be a far safer option to use a ground or distance line to be able to return to your start point. □

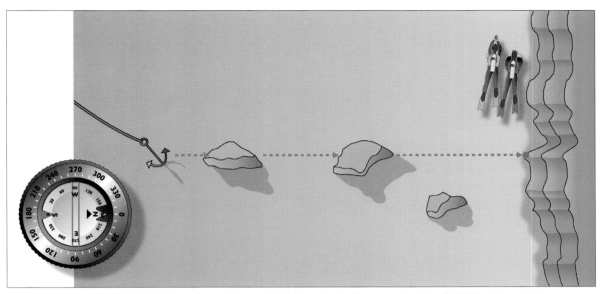

Knowing the shot has been dropped due south of the reef, the divers set a bearing of 360° (north) on their compasses. Sighting the first prominent object on that bearing at the limit of their visibility, they swim to it and take a new sighting. This process is repeated until they reach the reef. Returning from the same point on the reef they can use a compass bearing of 180° (south) to retrace the route.

Chapter five

Skills and equipment

As a diver you should always aim to extend your experience, and this will invoke the use of extra equipment. You will need to acquire skills to use this equipment effectively. Ropes, reels, lines and buoys can make your diving safer and more precise and will become essential items in your kit bag. Other pieces of equipment such as underwater cameras can be used to take your diving into completely new areas of enjoyment.

Skills and equipment
Ropes and knots

A bowline

A reef knot

For the enthusiast there are books devoted solely to knots, how to tie them and when to use them. Here, we concentrate on those most commonly used by divers.

The bowline: probably the knot most well known to divers, the bowline is used to form a loop or eye in a length of rope. It is not difficult to tie and is easy to undo as long as it is not under load.

The reef knot: again very well known, and frequently misused. The reef knot is for tying two ends of a line around an object such as the neck of a sack or a parcel. Probably most relevant to a diver in first aid, tying a bandage or sling. It is neither strong enough nor reliable enough to be used for tying two lines together to obtain a greater length.

The clove hitch: a quick and simple way of making fast a boat or tender, easy to adjust and undo if not loaded, it is not secure enough for long-term unattended use.

The anchor hitch or fisherman's bend: as its name implies used to connect anchor and line, also a good knot to use for tying off shot weights and buoys.

The single sheet bend: used to temporarily tie two lines together usually of different diameters, typically a light heaving line and a heavier mooring line. A close cousin to the bowline.

The double sheet bend: similar to the single sheet bend but more secure.

A clove hitch

An anchor hitch or fisherman's bend

A single sheet bend

A double sheet bend

A round turn and two half hitches

A figure-of-eight knot

Round turn and two half hitches: used to secure a rope to fixtures such as a bollard.

The figure-of-eight knot: a stop knot placed in the end of a line, usually to stop in running through an eye.

Types of rope

A karabiner

Close up of the lay of a rope

The karabiner: by far the best way of connecting lines to other objects or lines in or underwater are spring-loaded metal clips such as the karabiner or snap-link. As rope seems to have a mind of its own as soon as it is immersed, the sensible diver ensures that in-water rope handling and knot tying is kept to an absolute minimum. Wherever possible the work is performed in advance on the surface and in-water operations are restricted to the use of karabiners.

Types of rope: normal rope consists of three strands wound together with a right handed twist, or 'lay'. Because of this twist, knots tied in right-hand laid rope may have different properties if they are tied 'left handed', possibly causing them to slip. The twist also means there is a right and a wrong way to coil such rope. Coiling against the lay will cause a twist to form with each coil that is made, resulting in tangling problems. Braided rope, consisting of straight running strands as a load-bearing central core, protected by an outer woven sleeve are much less prone to kinking. Where braided ropes are used in circumstances where load bearing is critical, follow manufacturers' advice regarding the rope's working life. It is important to

keep all ropes clean and uncontaminated by chemicals or abrasive agents such as sand grains, especially braided cordage. This is because the crucial central core of the rope is not open to inspection, wear is hidden and potentially dangerous deterioration is hidden from view. Woven tapes or straps which are less prone to kinking and tangling problems also have uses in diving, especially where short, fixed lengths are needed. While traditional knots may by inappropriate there are a number of specialised fittings such as auto-lock karabiners and connector clips that we can borrow from the mountaineering and caving world.

Anchor lines

This short text is not designed in any way to qualify you as a sailor, merely to discuss some aspects of boating equipment as it impinges on diving. The type and weight of anchor chosen to moor a boat will vary according to the size of the boat and the nature of the sea bed at that location. The anchor rope is likely to be at least 15mm in diameter and will probably have a few metres of chain to help keep the anchor at the right angle to the sea bed, enhancing its holding properties.

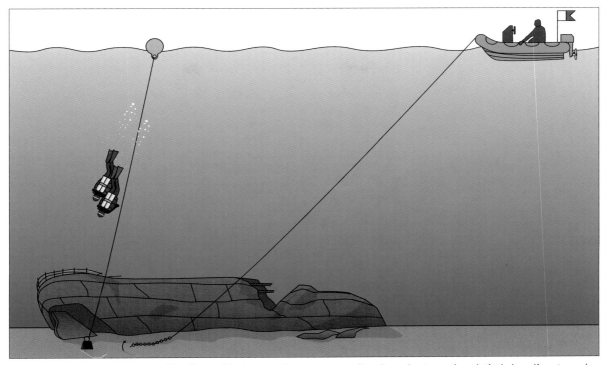

Descending a shot-line provides divers with the most direct route to a dive site as boats require relatively long lines to ancho
securely. Shot-lines can also provide decompression or safety-stop facilities leaving the cover boat freedom of movement

When a boat is at anchor, most sailors would want a length of anchor line paid out equivalent to up to seven times the depth of water. If the anchor is dropped at the dive site and the anchor line used to guide the divers, this would mean at a 20m-deep site the divers would be swimming about 150m, a considerable expenditure of effort, breathing gas and underwater time. As the dive boat will not be left unattended and sea conditions will be reasonable to permit diving, most dive boats would anchor with between two and three times the depth of water. However, this still increases the distance the divers have to swim, so is not ideal, especially on deeper dives.

Shot-lines

A standard shot-line is a very simple assembly consisting of a weight, a length of line and a buoy. Its purpose is to both mark the dive site and to provide

the shortest route for the divers to arrive there from the surface. Given the variability of sea conditions, this basic simple shot-line may not suffice. Firstly, even on a specific site, tidal variations will cause depth changes and in many instances the same shot is used to mark a number of sites with different depths. Unless the length of the shot is suitably adjusted, it is not going to be the right length every time and consequently not provide the best route for the divers. A number of complex pulley-type systems have been employed to try to achieve automatic minimum-length adjustment but have rarely proved successful in real-life conditions. Divers are also notoriously reluctant to cut lengths of line and frequently resort to untidy coils of excess rope floating dangerously around the buoy at the surface, or even worse around the weight at the bottom of the line. The alternative of having a shot-line that is the right length for the deepest dive but provides an ever-lengthening diagonal path as it

Shot-lines

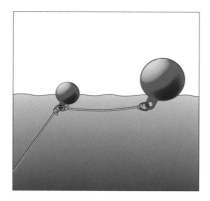

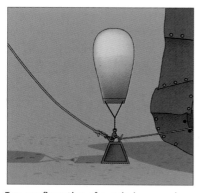

Top, configuration of a main buoy used in conjunction with a smaller signal buoy; above, the shot is attached to the wreck by a short length of relatively weak 'sacrificial' line which can be snapped when the shot is finally recovered by the surface party. This system can help counteract any tendency of the shot to drift during the dive because of wind, wave or current action. The small lifting bag can be inflated to make recovery of the shot easier at the end of the dive

is used on progressively shallower sites is rather missing the point.

The only solution is to have a shot-line that is quickly and simply and accurately adjustable by divers in a boat to allow use in a variety of depths. One effective solution is to use a number of pre-prepared rope lengths or 'strops' with each end terminated in an eye or a karabiner. Typically a boat would carry a range of such lengths, say 30, 20, 10, 5 and 2m to enable a shot-line of suitable length to be quickly clipped together as the boat arrives on site and the actual depth is verified by echo sounder. To provide even finer adjustment and to help absorb wave action, many divers include a 3–5m length of small, boat anchor chain between the bottom of the line and the weight.

The role of a shot-line means it can make the difference between a successful dive or a total failure, so it is not wise to cut corners in either its construction or use. Firstly it must be easy to handle, even in a small, well-loaded dive inflatable. There is a world of handling difference between the cheap polypropylene three-strand laid rope and a luxurious braided nylon or terylene. Given the longer life and greater ease of deployment and recovery, the price difference can soon be justified. As it will be used by the divers as a down line, the diameter needs to be substantial, 15mm is commonly chosen. The bottom weight also needs to be considered in this light. The heavier the weight the faster it will sink, which helps to make site marking more accurate. Another consideration is the possibility of groups of divers performing fixed decompression stops on the shot-line, in which case the weight may well need to be on the heavier side. However, a balance must be struck with the problems of transporting and recovering large weights and typically a weight of between 15 and 25kg is employed. As an alternative, particularly for wreck diving, the use of a small folding anchor or an anchor made with deliberately weak tines (hooks made from 10mm rebar which will straighten when pulled hard), may be considered.

Given the size of the weight and nature of the rope an appropriately sized buoy can be chosen. This also needs to be easily visible to a patrolling cover boat, so the colour also needs to be considered. To cope with errors in depth estimation or situations such as pinnacle or large wreck sites where the shot may become displaced into deeper waters, the buoy must be able to easily support the shot-line weight and that of any decompressing divers. A buoyancy of 50kg is commonly used.

Some divers employ a slightly more sophisticated system consisting of two buoys, a large main 'floater' and a smaller 'signal' buoy. The signal buoy, often of around 10kg buoyancy, is clipped in at the correct shot-line length and a further 3–5m of line allowed before the main buoy is attached. When deployed in a current, the signal buoy is usually pulled under water and only the main buoy remains visible. As the tide slacks off, the weaker current allows the signal buoy to surface indicating conditions are then diveable. Should the shot drag into deeper water, this system has the added advantage of signalling the fact to the boat cover by the disappearance of the smaller buoy. With both buoys on the surface, provided the wind is not strong, any separation of the two buoys can give an indication of current strength and direction.

'Lazy' shot decompression stations. These are attached to the main shot during the dive but once all the divers have arrived at the decompression station they can be detached and allowed to drift with the current (as shown above) so making the stop more comfortable for the divers. Large buoys are used both to support the decompression station and make it easy for the surface cove boat to follow

For wreck diving it is often either not possible or not desirable to put the shot directly into the wreck and instead it is dropped as close as possible to the site. To assist following groups the first pair down will then either move the shot-line right up to the wreck or run out a guide line. In circumstances where the shot-line might be pulled away from the site by current or divers pulling themselves down the line (not encouraged!), a weak breakable and sacrificial length of line is sometimes used to attach the shot to the wreck.

To assist recovery of the shot at the end of the dive various techniques are employed. The last pair of divers may have the task of moving the shot clear of any entanglements. Large shot weights may have a lifting bag attached which can be partially inflated to help recovery, folding anchors can be folded and locked in that configuration. Sometimes the dive plan will call for the shot to be so freed and set in drifting

mode to make decompression in a current more comfortable, a technique often referred to as a lazy shot. Of course, it is important before these operations are carried out to be sure that no divers wanting to return to the shot-line are still at the site. This is often controlled by means of signing arrival and departure on a slate attached at the bottom of the shot, or a system of removeable tags.

Preparing to ascend

A diver using a reel to deploy a buoy mid-water

Divers' reels

Many divers consider a small reel wound with between 30 and 75m of 2–3mm braided high-visibility line an essential part of their personal diving equipment. The reel usually has a ratchet mechanism for deploying the line which can be locked when a desired length has been paid out. Ideally carried stowed in an easily accessible BC pocket and clipped by a short lanyard to the diver to prevent loss, the reel and line can be used in a variety of situations.

Surface marker buoy: the line is clipped to a buoy of sufficient size to be difficult for a pair of divers to inadvertently pull it below the surface and big and bright enough to be easily visible to people on the surface, typically around 15kg is used with 10kg regarded as a minimum. While bigger may be thought better, a balance has to be struck with the problems caused by drag against wind and water. Some styles incorporate a diving flag to help distinguish the

surface marker buoy (SMB) from fishermen's floats. In use the line is paid out as the divers descend and while it is impractical to tow with the line vertical it is best to allow the minimum amount of line that is comfortable to tow. In low visibility the buddy may also hold or even attach to the line, using it as a buddy line. Ascents are made using the reeling in of the line to help control ascent speed and halting the process when precautionary or decompression stops are reached.

DSMB line: many divers consider a reel the best way of deploying a delayed surface marker buoy (DSMB), even to the extent of carrying a second dedicated reel. The DSMB should be considered an essential piece of safety equipment. It can play an important location role in resolving diver separation or lost ascent line situations. Before inflating the DSMB make sure the line brake is released on the reel and the reel is not attached to the diver. If the ascent is 'free' the DSMB

Divers' reels

The circular search is very popular as it is simple to set up and perform. The dive team is positioned along the reel line and a marker laid to indicate the sweep start (and end) point. Following each complete circular sweep more line is deployed and the marker repositioned before the next sweep is conducted

This simple arrangement of a weight, short line and plastic bottle can be used to accurately mark underwater positions, such as the beginning of a search sweep

may be deployed at depth – the line can be used to guide the ascent and is reeled in as you ascend so giving some idea of ascent speed. If the ascent is using an anchor or shot-line and DSMB deployment is signalling arrival at a stop, then there is less risk of entanglement if it is deployed at the stop depth.

Bottom, distance or wreck line: the line end is either fixed near or clipped to the bottom of the shot-line and the line deployed as the diver explores the site, providing a guideline back to the ascent route. The line should be kept fairly taut to help avoid snagging.

Some general observations on the use of reels and lines must include the advice to always carry an easily accessible diving knife with a sharp, serrated edge suitable for cutting the lines you are using.

Ensure that any line attached to you is fastened with a quick-release mechanism that is easily reached and

operated whether the line is in use, under tension or just being carried. While it is important to avoid losing your delayed SMB during deployment it is even more important that it is not attached to you as any unexpected line problem could then result in an uncontrolled buoyant ascent.

Underwater search techniques

In principle, searching for objects underwater is not very different from the same activity on land, once the differences in environment, mobility and visibility are accounted for. The size of the missing object may well be thought an issue and usually does have a major impact on the likelihood of success, but it can sometimes be as difficult to find a shipwreck as a wedding ring lost from a jetty. What is really important is a methodical approach to both the planning and conduct of the operation. Given a diver's limited

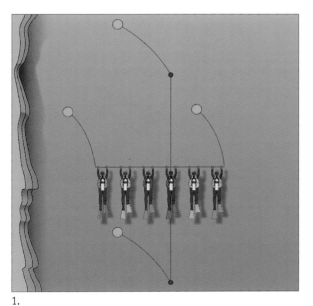

1.

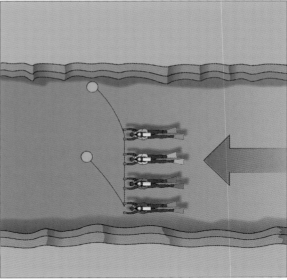

2.

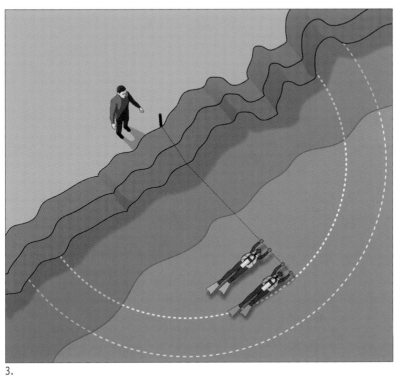

3.

Here are some examples of search techniques:

1. A guide line (laid from the surface) is used for a team of divers, connected by a signalling line, to follow.

2. A similar technique which can be employed where there are natural constraints to the area such as river banks.

3. A semi-circular search method that can easily be employed, using a distance line, to search outwards from a shoreline reference point.

Lifting techniques

range in both time and distance, it is important that searching is effective and efficient and that as much work as can be is performed at the surface.

The first essential is to identify as accurately as possible the suspected location of the missing object. To this end it is worth observing that if you are present when an object is lost you should take immediate steps to identify the location, such as 'man overboard' position recording with an active GPS, deploying a shot-line and buoy or taking visual transits. When conducting the search the divers need as short a path as possible down to the suspected point of the loss in order to maximise underwater search time.

When searching underwater it is important that all normal safety guidelines are followed with due attention being paid to decompression requirements and buddy-diving procedures. It is essential to mark the start point of the search, a function performed by the shot weight. It is also important to know exactly where you have searched, as excessive overlap of search areas is needlessly inefficient. Cheap but effective underwater markers can be fashioned from a small weight, a metre or so of line and a plastic bottle inflated just enough to raise the line vertically but not lift it from the bottom. Such markers can be placed to indicate the extent of an already searched area or the start point on the outer radius of a circular search.

A range of underwater techniques may be employed, depending largely on factors such as the number and skill level of available divers, the underwater visibility, the nature of the bottom and the size of the lost object. It is usual to employ rope or line to help either delineate the search area or provide directional guidance to the divers. This may take the form of specially prepared lines, possibly equipped with weights and marker buoys, or may just be the reels and wreck lines of the participating divers. Whichever system is used, divers are placed along the search line in a spacing to maintain visual contact but maximise the area covered. Rope signals can be used for communication but normal buddy observation should not be abandoned in the excitement of the work. In searching the designated area all possible steps should be taken to avoid stirring up silt, either by the divers themselves or movement from the lines they are employing. Don't forget to keep a careful eye on gauges and dive time and have some method of buoying or marking the object when it is found.

Lifting techniques

Having found your missing object you will want to recover it and return it to its rightful owner. A lost watch or ring is not going to pose a problem, but an outboard engine is not something you can casually swim up to the surface. Beware of lifting heavy objects to the surface using your personal buoyancy, be it drysuit or BC. Should you let go of the object you are perfectly set up for an uncontrolled and rapid buoyant ascent. Even hanging on to the object and finning can create difficulties through excessive breathing-gas consumption, exhaustion or inability to control personal buoyancy because both hands are occupied.

The simplest solution is to securely fasten a strong enough line to the object and recover it to the surface from a boat, which may be equipped with a winch that is designed for this purpose. The lift may be assisted by tying and inflating a lifting bag to the object.

Indeed, the whole lift may be conducted using one or more lifting bags, but this is going to need a certain amount of pre-planning and knowledge regarding the nature of the object to be raised. Unfortunately, it also involves a little mathematics. Put simply, to make the object float you need to add an amount of buoyancy that will equal (and slightly exceed) its mass in the water. As 1 litre of water has a mass of 1kg, displacing 1 litre of water in an airtight container such as a drum or lifting bag with air will provide a lift of 1kg. So a 25-litre container filled with air will provide 25kg of lift. We now need to recall the effects of pressure on volumes of gas at depth. If we were to fill this 25-litre container with air at a depth of 10m, the air would be at a pressure of 2 bar and would want to expand to twice its volume by the time it reached the 1-bar ambient pressure at the surface. That could have catastrophic effects on the container if there was no means for the air to escape as it tried to expand, so a container used in this way should never be sealed.

Looking at the calculation in a different way, we can also note that to fill the 25kg container with air at 2-bar pressure will require some 50 litres of air at surface pressure. A 10-litre dive cylinder filled to 200 bar contains 2,000 litres of 'free' air, so could be used to fill (2,000 / 50) 40 of these containers at 10m. Repeating the exercise at a depth of 30m, with a 4-bar ambient pressure, we would need (4 x 25) 100 litres of 'free' air to fill the same container and our dive cylinder would only fill (2,000 / 100) 20 containers. It is worth noting that attaching your 10-litre personal lifting bag to help lift the anchor at the end of the dive and inflating it just half full will consume (4 x 5) 20 litres of your air supply. Returning to the recovery of sunken articles, we can choose between rigid containers such as plastic or metal drums, or flexible containers such as lifting bags. Today's preference is for lifting bags as they are relatively cheap, designed for the job and much easier for a diver to carry to the site, attach and inflate.

All underwater objects displace some of the water they are submerged in. This displaced water creates an up-thrust on the object equal to the mass of the displaced water. So, if a sunken object has a volume of 100 litres it will displace 100 litres of water, creating an up-thrust of 100kg, effectively lightening the object by 100kg as long as it remains submerged. Knowing the volume of a sunken object is often not simple. If it is constructed of a single material, such as steel, timber or concrete (or gold!) and the mass is known then the volume may be calculated using the density of the material. For example, to lift a steel structure with a mass of 1000kg, knowing steel has a density of 7,850kg / m3, we can calculate its volume to be (1,000 / 7,850) 0.127 m3 or (1,000 x 0.127) 127 litres. This means underwater it will experience an up-thrust of 127kg and we need only supply (1,000 – 127) 873kg of buoyancy. Sometimes sunken objects settle well into the sea bed which can cause initial 'sticking', especially if the bottom is mud. Extra buoyancy may then be required to initiate the lift which can cause rapid acceleration once the lift commences.

Having calculated the required buoyancy, some means of providing the appropriate volume of air is needed at the depth of the object. If the volume is significant it will be best to use a hose from a surface compressor. There is no need for a very high-pressure appliance, the type encountered on building sites is satisfactory for large projects, one used for paint spraying may suffice for smaller lifts. Alternatively diving cylinders may be sufficient and convenient, but using your own breathing-gas supply should be done with caution. Make sure you can afford to lose the volume required to lift the object. When inflating lifting bags, especially smaller ones, with your secondary regulator be careful not to allow the regulator to become trapped inside the bag when the neck tightens as the bag inflates.

In common with other underwater tasks, it is important to do as much preparation on the surface before the underwater phase of the lift commences. A method of attaching the buoyancy must be thought

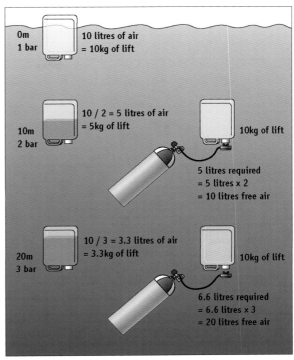

If an open container holding 10 litres of air is taken from the surface to 10m, the doubled pressure will reduce the volume of air to 5 litres. As it then only displaces 5 litres of water its lift is reduced from 10kg to 5kg. If 10 litres of air (occupying 5 litres at that depth) is added, the container will again be full and displace 10 litres of water, providing 10kg of lift. If the container was taken straight from the surface to 20m the threefold pressure increase would reduce the volume of air to 3.3 litres, requiring some 20 litres of free air to again fill the container

out and prepared. Not surprisingly, specialist strops and cables used in lifting on the surface are frequently the preferred solution underwater. It is vital that any attachment is easily capable of bearing the load placed upon it, something that also applies to the attachment point on the object being lifted. The desired attitude of the object when it is lifted must be considered and the attachment point or method chosen to produce this positioning. For larger objects, to obtain a safe lift and a suitable attitude it may be necessary to spread the lift over a number of attachment points, using several lifting bags.

Lifting techniques

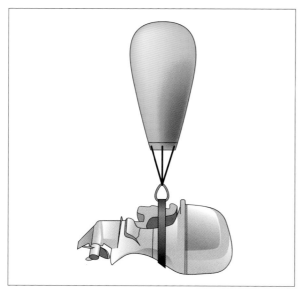

This outboard engine weighs about 200kg submerged so will need a lift bag with some 200 litres capacity. At a depth of 30m the pressure of 4 bar means (4 x 200) 800 litres of air will be needed. This equates to 40 per cent of a 10-litre cylinder filled to 200 bar.

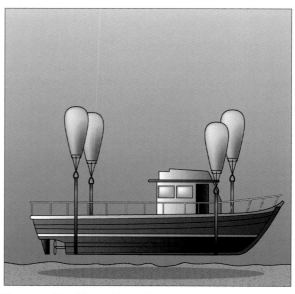

When attaching lift to objects, be sure the attaching points can withstand the force that will be applied when the lift occurs. Ensure that strops used to spread lifting forces are secure and will not move and that the lift is applied so the object remains stable

There is always a problem fine tuning the amount of lift provided to the amount of lift needed, having a lifting bag that exactly matches the underwater mass of the object is rare. Using too large a lifting bag will certainly start the lift process, but as the ascent proceeds and the air in the bag expands, the assembly will accelerate and it is very easy for matters to get out of control. Lifting bags can arrive at the surface travelling so fast they can temporarily capsize, losing sufficient air for everything to sink back to the sea bed. Such uncontrolled lifts can pose a danger to the surface cover, which should stand off the site when the lift commences, and to the divers below, who should also move away. Lifting bags have also been known to burst, as the expansion rate has been too great to allow the excess air to escape through the neck. For this reason many lifting bags are fitted with over-pressure relief valves.

A good technique is to use a lifting bag which is just too small for the job in hand and to supplement it with a smaller bag that will add the extra buoyancy needed. The main bag is filled completely at the bottom and the trimming bag then initiates the lift. When the air in this bag expands to fill it completely the buoyancy change is small enough not to cause any

problems. An alternative is to use lifting bags fitted with a manual relief valve, often operated by means of a lanyard. A diver can then ascend with the bag, carefully controlling the ascent rate by releasing excess air as needed. It must be emphasised that this is not a simple task and the diver must never exceed safe personal ascent rates or omit stops just for the sake of the lift. The risks of a diver being entangled and dragged up during the lift or trapped as a result of a failed lift must always be taken into consideration and measures taken to avoid such occurrences.

With the lifting bags at the surface the recovery is not complete and the object will be suspended some metres below the surface. Careful thought must be given as to whether it can be manhandled or craned onto the boat, or lashed alongside or towed back to the shore. Getting the object aboard can be a tricky operation because once tension is taken off the lifting bags and the object raised, the bags can capsize and lose air. Should the recovery not succeed the object no longer has any buoyancy and can easily be lost back to the sea bed. If towing is chosen then either it must be done carefully and slowly so as not to capsize the lifting bags or more permanent buoyancy added for the tow. An advantage here of using drums for

Divers using rebreathers require proper training

the lift is that they can often be sealed once at the surface providing more secure buoyancy for the tow. Often drums may also be attached more closely to the object, making it float higher in the water causing less problems of excessive draft when the shore or harbour is eventually reached.

Rebreathers

While on the subject of the different types of equipment that divers use, it is worth looking at the role of the rebreather in recreational diving.

The main thrust of development in breathing apparatus has long been on the relatively simple open-circuit breathing system firstly based on the Cousteau/Gagnan twin-hose regulator and then on the two-stage single hose derivatives of this equipment. These systems are referred to as open circuit because the exhaled gas from the diver is exhausted to surrounding water and included in this exhaust gas is a proportion of oxygen. The principle of the rebreather is simply to recycle this unused oxygen rather than waste it, and to keep the level topped up automatically from the breathing-gas supply whenever the level drops so low as to become of no value to the diver.

The main problem to solve is that the oxygen we do use in the metabolic process is exhaled as carbon dioxide and if this was kept in this closed-circuit breathing cycle would poison the diver. To remove the carbon dioxide the exhaled gas is passed through a 'scrubber', where it is chemically removed. The remaining gas is then recycled with the oxygen content, periodically being topped up as it is used. This is a very crude and simplistic description of a process that demands highly complex equipment, previously the domain of only the military or leading-edge commercial divers. However, today's sophisticated micro-technology and engineering are bringing sufficiently reliable rebreathers into the recreational divers reach – but that is another book...

It is worth making a few points on the interaction of open circuit and rebreather divers. It is always best to pair divers according to experience, interest and equipment. The equipment differences between open circuit and rebreather divers means pairing them together requires a number of extra factors to be considered. As the main point of buddy diving is mutual support it is important that the equipment configuration of both divers allows that to happen. Both must carry an alternate air source that will

Marine animals make superb photographic subjects

Using a housed camera

Photographing a gorgonian fan

serve either themselves or their buddy in the event of either having a primary breathing source failure. It is important that this alternate air source supply is sufficient for the pair to achieve a safe return to the surface, including any necessary decompression stops.

To provide full support, dive buddies must understand each other's equipment and its operation. Attendance on a rebreather familiarisation course will help any open-circuit diver better fulfil their role, the same point applying to the dive marshal, who will need to understand that the rebreather diver's underwater position will not be marked by bubbles on the surface. It cannot be over-emphasised that all divers using rebreathers require special training regarding their use, and this is even more important in regard to previous open-circuit divers as a number of techniques have to be completely re-learned.

Photography/videography

Photographers are compelled to use high technology to capture the ever-changing marine life, the mood of a shipwreck, the special effects of underwater lighting or even the strange, zero-gravity forms created by their underwater companions. To allow for this requires good dive planning, so be prepared. You may need to act as model, breathing out on demand, adopt and hold impossible positions, defying current and the turning actions of your equipment. Spending what seems like an age as an underwater lighting assistant for a picture that is snapped in a fraction of a second, swimming past a piece of wreckage innumerable times until the sequence is finally captured, does not make dive leading photographers easy.

Reversing roles does not make life any simpler, as being a dive leader and a photographer simultaneously is not an easy marriage. Keeping track of a buddy through the viewfinder of a camera is not easy – unless they are the subject at the time. The difficulty is overcoming the temptation to become too task oriented and lose sight of the duties of dive leading. Of course, this applies to all diving pursuits not just photography, but it is important that dive leaders do not compromise their responsibilities while pursuing other interests. Pre-settable time and depth alarms on dive computers can help, but must not be a substitute for proper vigilance. The best answer is not to mix the two, avoid being a photographer and dive leading at

Diver propulsion vehicles

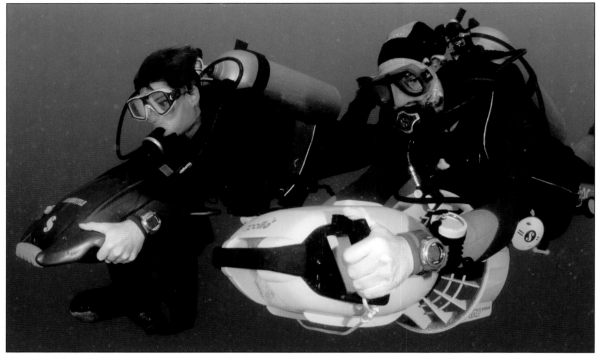

Diver propulsion vehicles can reduce the amount of energy a diver expends

the same time, and make sure photographer's buddies are well-briefed, patient divers, fully understanding and content with their roles. With today's digital equipment stunning results can be obtained. The ability to view results immediately, even underwater, and re-shoot in the same conditions can make the photographer's learning curve so much shorter and the results greatly improved. Ultimately, though, sharing the pleasure of well shot or filmed underwater records can be a good recompense for the photographer's buddy.

Diver propulsion vehicles

To extend our travelling capabilities on land, mankind has developed a variety of vehicles. The same situation pertains underwater. To penetrate great depths we have the bathyscaphe and a variety of submarines for shallow and intermediate depths. Of most interest to

the diver are systems that enable us to cover a greater area in the depth range we habitually operate in, using normal recreational diving equipment.

The simplest of these are the hydroplanes or planning boards towed behind a surface craft. These devices are essentially small 'wings' equipped with handles for the divers to hold onto which are connected to the cover boat by around 50m of tow line. Pulled at a slow speed, 1–3 knots, the divers can control the attitude of the hydrofoil, making it 'fly' through the water at any desired depth. Care must be taken with descent and ascent speeds and thought given to equipment configuration to enable gauges to be monitored. Looking sideways or travelling too fast can easily result in masks flooding or being swept off and even regulators pulled out of mouths. Should the divers release the device this is normally obvious to the towing vessel and the hydrofoil normally planes to the surface. If an interesting site has been discovered the divers can mark this by using a mini-shot and can also ascend deploying their personal delayed SMBs.

Using a hydrofoil means most of the directional control lies with the surface party. By using an independent diver propulsion vehicle (DPV), autonomy is given back to the diver. DPVs come in two main varieties, the homemade 'wet' submarine type and the commercially produced 'tugs'. The wet submarines are often modelled on the military two-man torpedo or chariot style, the divers often sitting astride a cylinder containing batteries and a motor, driven by a rear propeller and controlling attitude by hydroplanes. Some highly sophisticated machines have been constructed and enthusiasts have formed associations which organise international meets.

Several manufacturers produce commercially available models in the form of one-diver tugs, a small, streamlined plastic housing containing battery and motor with a shielded propeller. The diver holds onto two handles which also contain a 'deadman' throttle control. On some models with rear handles the diver streams behind the unit, on others with forward handles the unit lies below the diver, but in both direction is controlled by the diver's attitude and fin positioning. As speed is directly controlled by the diver much more comfortable rides can be enjoyed. Given two such machines normal buddy diving procedures may be adopted.

Emergency signalling – general and personal

As your diving experience develops, so does the opportunity to dive more and more adventurous sites. To explore these sites with the minimum of extra risk prudent divers, and especially dive leaders, adopt a number of extra techniques and procedures, among them being a selection of communication systems. The two main communication channels available to divers are sight and sound and the major difficulty to overcome is distance. Underwater, the distance we are mostly concerned with is between diving buddies, while on the surface it is either diver to cover party or in extreme situations to emergency services. Signalling underwater is normally visual and is limited by local visibility. Sound can be used to attract attention, but if visual contact is absent it is difficult underwater to allocate a direction to a sound. Popular sound generation methods are shouting (usually through the regulator), banging a knife butt on the diving cylinder, tapping on the cylinder with a plastic bead held there by an bungee band or sounding a compressed air horn operated by the medium-pressure BC hose.

At the surface, shouting, blowing the whistle found attached to most BCs, operating a compressed air horn (but not too near your ear) can all be employed. However, sound at the surface can have a limited range, especially if the divers are downwind of the cover boat and have to compete with boat engine and compressor noise. As the cover boat should be keeping a good lookout for surfacing divers, visual methods may well be the most effective. Spotting divers at the surface is difficult because not much more than the head protrudes and these can be hidden by waves for much of the time. A variety of target enhancement techniques can be employed. To maximise the chance of spotting the head, contrasting Day-Glo coloured hoods can be worn. Your personal SMB/DSMB will also help. Many divers carry a rolled up signalling flag with an extendable handle attached by bungee bands to their diving cylinder. This can be quickly and easily assembled at the surface and produces a flag which can be waved a metre or more above the diver, greatly enhancing the chance of them being spotted. Signalling mirrors have long been used for attracting attention over long distances when sunshine is present. The wide prevalence of compact discs today means it is easy for a diver to carry a CD in a BC pocket and use the shiny side to try to beam reflected light at the surface party.

More extreme signalling devices may also be carried by divers, including waterproof pyrotechnics. Mini-flare guns can fire various coloured flares up to 60m high, the flare burning for six seconds at 3,000 candlepower making it visible up to 8km away. The gun is usually supplied in a plastic pack containing eight flares and in some countries ownership requires a firearms permit. Special day/night flares that are waterproof to 30m are also available. These handheld double-ended devices consist of a red flare at one end and an orange smoke generator at the other. Water and pressure-proof containers are available to extend depth resistance to 150m. Carrying any pyrotechnic devices is generally forbidden by airlines.

More sophisticated are the present-day range of electronic signalling devices that may be carried by the diver. These can range from a simple VHF radio carried in a waterproof container to emergency signalling beacons communicating with the rescue services by

A surface marker buoy is highly visible

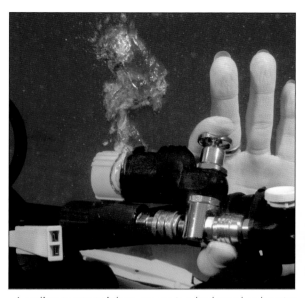

A medium-pressure air horn can create a loud sound underwater or at the surface, but care should be taken not to use one too close to people's ears

A flag is another means of signalling

satellite. VHF radio transmitter/receivers with a range of 3km are now available with built-in GPS receivers, enabling paired units to exchange positions and display range and direction to each other. Emergency Position Indicating Radio Beacons (EPIRB) are small radio transmitters which when activated transmit a signal directly to the emergency services. The emergency services can calculate a search position and rescue vessels or aircraft can use the EPIRB signal to home in on the casualty. A range of EPIRBs have been produced and marketed, the smaller cheaper models of most interest to divers have subsequently caused so many false alerts overloading the emergency services that they are no longer effective in producing a rapid response, service is being withdrawn and purchase no longer recommended. Newer devices transmit a unique serial number linked to an owner enabling emergency services to rapidly validate alerts. Many of these units also have built in GPS units enabling a position fix accurate to within 15m to be transmitted.

Besides lost diver direct emergency service contact, cover boats may also need to communicate with emergency services. This will normally be achieved by marine radio although in coastal regions even mobile phones have been used. Emergency services always prefer to be contacted as early as possible, even to be alerted to the possibility of an incident developing to a stage where outside support might be required. When contacting them make sure all details regarding the situation are to hand, particularly as accurate a position as possible and nature of the incident and details of the casualty. In decompression incidents, unless otherwise obvious, most emergency services will assume the dive buddy may also require treatment and transportation to recompression facilities. □

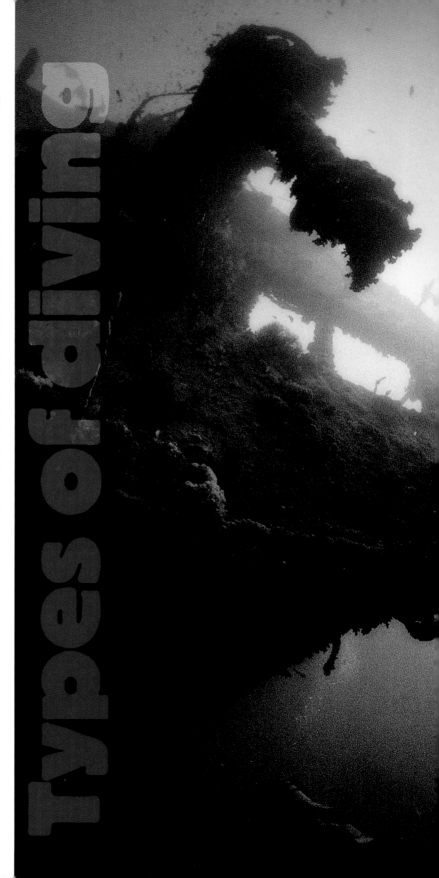

Chapter six

Types of diving

Now that you've reached a suitably high level of diving experience, the opportunity to enjoy a variety of different types of diving presents itself. Wreck diving is one of the most popular forms of diving, combining history with marine biology in a uniquely engaging form. Drift diving can add an invigorating edge to your diving experience, while ice and cave diving will require substantial extra training, allowing you the chance to enjoy further adventure as you explore less-trodden dive paths.

Types of diving
Drift diving

Drift diving allows for a wider range of exploration

While the normal range of a diver underwater is fairly restricted, there is one very simple way of extending it – let the water do the work. Tides and currents are often a problem for the diver who is trying to remain in a specific area. If you can free yourself from these constraints, a new and exiting diving experience is at hand. Allowing the current to do the hard work, you can truly fly above the sea bed – a weightless observer of the underwater world. There are, of course, limitations to this submarine freedom. At some stage the flight must finish and it is more than useful to have a cover boat waiting for you at the surface. Therefore, some planning will be called for to avoid the risk of divers separating from each other and their surface cover.

In order for the boat to follow your underwater journey, it must have something visible to follow. Requirement number one is an SMB (surface marker buoy), to mark each diving pair. The second requirement is that if the divers are to drift, there must be a current. Some homework with a chart, tide tables and possibly some local knowledge should enable a suitable tidal current to be found. It should be in an area that avoids surface obstructions such as mooring buoys, fishermen's pots or other lines and areas of turbulent water that create a 'washing machine' effect where divers will be unable to control their buoyancy.

On drift dives divers should carry DSMBs in the event of buddy separation

Towing an SMB makes it far easier for a support boat to stay in contact with the divers

You should only attempt a drift dive when there is good surface visibility to allow the surface cover to keep the divers' SMB in sight at all times. Rain, mist or a heavy swell will mean the strong possibility of surface cover losing sight of the divers. The next question is one of position and timing, ascertaining just where will be the best entry point and when will be the best time. Having some estimation of the speed is useful. Don't be over-ambitious – 1 to 1.5 knots is ample for a first drift dive. It can be very difficult for a cover boat to follow and support more than one group of divers at a time. Even if groups set off together, it is easy for one group to get into an eddy and drift at a different speed or direction than another. For a buddy pair sharing an SMB, staying together should not be a problem. Plan to enter the water together and stay together on the dive. If one diver stops to look at something while holding onto a rock without warning his or her buddy, the buddy will continue to drift onwards. This will require hard finning to catch up and, depending on the current, may mean diver separation by some considerable distance. If divers are concerned about separation they can use the SMB line as a buddy line. One diver holds and controls the reel and the other holds the line. Another method is to attach a separate line from the reel that the buddy can hold. However, should separation occur it is vital that both divers are quickly aware that it has occurred and follow normal separation surfacing procedures. Possible separation from each other requires that the buddy without the SMB carries his or her own surface detection aid such as a DSMB or dive flag.

As with all enjoyable and successful diving, good buoyancy control is essential and a careful lookout ahead is important. Though normally you will be swept clear of major obstacles by the current, you should keep a careful lookout for potential entanglement hazards. Low visibility and high-speed drifting do not mix well, and increase the risk of separation. A good dive plan is to finish the drift in shallower water, but a reasonably even depth site is the best choice. However, if depths vary and as currents can act vertically as well as horizontally, buoyancy control and decompression requirements need close observation. One other point to consider when drift diving is that 'flying' underwater requires little physical effort and additional thermal protection may need to be considered to prevent diver chilling.

Night diving

Night diving can be an unforgettable experience

Night diving

What on earth for? Well, it is certainly not just the 'Because it's there' rationale often attributed to mountaineers. For some people, diving at night is the most pleasurable of all types of diving. Exploring a site by night that you have dived so many times by day – a site you thought you knew backwards – reveals a totally new world. And not only a changed world, but one containing either strange and new inhabitants or familiar ones with totally new behaviour patterns. To extinguish your torch and survey your underwater world by moonlight and to wave your hand through the water and see the glowing, phosphorescent trail it leaves, are magical experiences all divers should try.

Night diving does make extra demands on the diver and surface cover. It involves extra planning, equipment and even a degree of technique adaptation. Firstly, in choosing the site, care must be taken that underwater navigation will not be too challenging, that it has good visibility, is current-free, well sheltered and with easily recognisable boundaries. Avoid areas where there is likely to be other surface traffic. An enclosed bay, a reef, a shallow wreck, even a pier or jetty, can fit these requirements and produce excellent night diving. Entry/exit points, whether boat or shore, need to be clearly marked by readily identifiable lights or lit objects and a check in/check out system utilised. With the visual restrictions of darkness, sound communication becomes even more important – sound tends to carry well over calm water. You should minimise unnecessary noise to make sure that any diver communications can be heard clearly.

No matter how bright the moon, some form of waterproof light is essential. Firstly, as a means of locating each diver, but also to best observe the night-time flora and fauna. One advantage of observing by torchlight is that the restricted field of vision focuses your attention on a smaller area, helping much more detail to be discovered. Illuminated only by torchlight,

A torch is an essential item of equipment when night diving

A battery powered light stick

colours invisible by day are revealed. To get the best out of the dive, make sure that you have a torch that is reasonably powerful and fitted with fresh or fully charged batteries. It is sensible to have a second torch as backup. A smaller torch that may be carried on all dives (for inspecting nooks and crannies) can suffice as a backup, but make sure it too has fresh batteries.

Try to prepare all your equipment in the light before the dive, and to kit up and buddy check with minimum light to preserve night vision. Contact and communication will be more difficult in the darkness. Often, night divers attach a 'light stick', either chemical or battery powered, to their SMBs or dive cylinders by means of a couple of rubber bands or cable ties. These light sticks can also be used to mark shot-lines or anchor ropes to help returning divers locate them. Light sticks are available in a number of colours, yellow and green being the most visible. Using these two colours, different buddy pairs may be identified by the surface cover, either simply by the two colours, by combinations of the colours, or by creating a pattern around the stick using a band of insulating tape. If you do use chemical light sticks, make sure they are disposed of in an environmentally friendly manner, the same point applying to used torch batteries.

Generally, back-up torches are attached to the BC and safely stowed in a pocket or clipped in place, while the main underwater lamp is carried in one hand, secured by a wrist lanyard. Head-mounted lamps are also available, ranging from simple headband models to the sophisticated helmet-mounted units favoured by cave divers. Try to avoid shining your torch into the eyes of your buddy and other divers or the surface party – you may destroy their night vision just as you need it! This is particularly difficult with head-mounted lamps. Strategic placing of reflective tape can make you more visible. Separation procedures must be carefully planned and agreed, and both divers must carry and be able to use a DSMB. A useful technique with some DSMBs to help surface location is to shine a torch up into or under the inflated buoy.

Moving around on land in the dark can be difficult and disorienting, but is certainly simpler if you know your surroundings. The same applies underwater, so it is best to night-dive sites that you are already familiar with in the daytime. On land you obtain a lot of positional information because your feet are in contact with the ground and you can see around you; underwater, this will be absent. Your weightless neutral buoyancy and limited awareness

A spider crab seen on a night dive

Night dives allow the chance to see nocturnal animals such as squid

A night dive will require good communication with your buddy

of underwater surroundings provides little feedback about your orientation and this can sometimes be a little disconcerting until you adapt. An experienced buddy is an important help as you climb the early part of the learning curve. You must, as on any dive, pay careful attention to the information provided by your gauges and/or computer. Some of these can be difficult to read, with torchlight reflecting off the face. Luminescent equipment can be 'charged' just before the dive by illuminating with it your torch and many computers provide a useful backlight option.

Descending some form of visible datum such as a shot-line, wall or slope, greatly helps both orientation and underwater position fixing and provides similar assistance for the ascent. Once at the bottom, keep off it! Many creatures hidden away during the day are out feeding at night, and colliding with sea urchins is bad for you and them. Control your buoyancy so that you hover above the bottom and make sure all your movements, especially arm and leg, are slow and careful. There is no need to travel great distances, indeed, navigation is much simpler if you don't. With many of the fish sleepy and docile, you can observe them in a manner which would be impossible by day. Moving slowly helps to maintain contact with your buddy, but you will need to communicate with them thoughtfully. Shining your torch directly in their eyes, which have become accustomed to the darkness, will cause a temporary 'night blindness'. Illuminate your hand signals to convey your message. If wanting to attract their attention shine your torch into the area they are observing and circle it slowly. Rapid torch movements are taken to indicate a problem. It is sensible to end the dive with a larger reserve than normal in case of separation from surface cover, so keep a careful watch on breathing-gas consumption. Pre-arrange with your buddy to pause near your ascent point and spend some time with your torches extinguished. Once your eyes become adjusted it is surprising just how much becomes visible and just how many biological light sources are present in the water. A gentle arm movement can trigger minute planktonic organisms to flash and glow, often providing a sparkling coating to temporarily outline your hand and arm. Surfacing procedures need to be planned in advance particularly the light signal to give to the surface cover to indicate that you have surfaced and all is well. These should be done without rapid torch movements, as again this is used to indicate a problem on the surface.

Types of diving   123

Deep diving

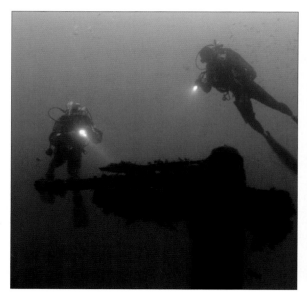

Deeper dives require careful planning and preparation

On deeper dives, divers need to pay even closer attention to their computers and contents gauges

Deep diving

It seems to be a basic human instinct to want to know and explore the limits. Mountaineers are challenged by the highest mountains and one of the commonest questions non-divers will pose is: 'How deep have you dived?' In relation to even the average depth of the oceans, honest answers are limited to: 'Not very deep at all,' but inevitably there is some kind of aura around the idea of exploring ever deeper.

So, the first thing to be done is to remove that aura. Deeper waters receive less light, which equates to less energy, so life forms are less abundant and temperatures are lower. Greater depth means greater distance from the surface, therefore there is a greater separation from the atmosphere we need for survival and other vital forms of surface support. Deeper depths mean greater pressure, bringing the added problems of gas toxicity, increased decompression penalties, narcosis problems and risk of DCI. It is certainly a diminishing returns situation, as useful bottom times become shorter while restrictive decompression stops increase. In short, rapture of the depth gauge is worth avoiding – diving to ever-increasing depths just for the sake of depth is not a rewarding activity.

However, there can be reasons for deep dives, and this time the reason is usually because something is there – there is a target that is otherwise not attainable. For example, the most intact wrecks tend to be in deeper waters. Here they are less subject to the violent wave-action of shallower waters, and the reduced oxygen content of the water means a slower rate of corrosion and consequent structural collapse. With the changed light and water properties, there are different life forms – certain flora and fauna can only be found in the deeper, darker zones. Sometimes it is the attraction of the geological formations, a deep cavern or pinnacle, that forms a focal point for certain fish or other undersea creatures. Whatever the reason, there can be valid reasons for exploring these limits, as long as the problems outlined above can be resolved and risks eliminated or reduced to sensible limits.

Specific issues such as narcosis and decompression are dealt with elsewhere in this volume, so here we can examine a more general strategy for deep diving. A good start is to try to quantify just what is understood by the word 'deep'. Obviously anything that is deeper than you have dived before needs this increase in depth to be taken into consideration as part of the planning process. What implications will the increase have for

The most intact wrecks tend to be found in deeper
waters

Deep diving

As depth increases natural illumination decreases and divers will require torches

your equipment needs, what new skills or knowledge will be needed? Certainly breathing-gas requirements and independent back-up gas supply must figure large in the plan. Maybe a different breathing gas is more appropriate. Will the dive cylinders you have been using contain sufficient breathing gas for the dive plus any necessary reserve? Will a pony cylinder be sufficient as a backup for the depth planned or would a twin-set be more appropriate? Will cooler waters demand a change in protective clothing? Changes in equipment will also have a knock-on effect by changing your buoyancy. Maybe access to the site will require a different kind of dive boat, which in turn demands further new skills and either diving or site location techniques. Plus, of course, the big issue of

decompression – will this be the first time you will experience a 'ceiling' and have to perform compulsory in-water decompression or will it be longer stops than you have done before that will require some form of decompression station or trapeze?

In considering these points, remember that increased experience is always easier to control and absorb when obtained in a progressive manner. Don't try to take on too many new tasks at once; familiarisation, practise or training with new equipment and techniques is best managed during shallower dives, where complete success might be less crucial and you have some performance latitude. Depth may be thought of as an amplifying factor for diving problems – anything that can be a setback on a shallow dive is likely to be a much bigger crisis if encountered at depth, so it is important to remove the likelihood of it occurring. Too-deep diving straight after a winter layoff is the root cause of many springtime diving incidents. Make sure that your equipment is functioning perfectly, your skills are in current practise and site conditions are well within limits.

The key to successful and enjoyable deeper diving is careful planning and preparation, taking all eventualities into account, with complete mastery of all the necessary skills before the event. That way you will start the dive in the right frame of mind and, hopefully, be better able to cope with the onset of nitrogen narcosis!

No clear surface

In your early diving experiences it is likely that you will have had nothing but water between you and the surface. However, as the number of sites you dive increases you will have the opportunity to swim under overhangs, to enter underwater caverns, and to explore the large, open interiors of sunken ships. In its simplest form following this type of no-clear-surface diving calls only for an awareness of the obstruction in order to avoid potentially damaging collisions that could be harmful to both the underwater environment and to yourself. As long as free access to open water is immediately accessible and visible, and the danger of entanglement is absent, having no clear surface is unlikely to cause any difficulty. Should any of these conditions not apply, then extra precautions will be needed. Cave diving and wreck diving are special cases that are covered later. For the moment, the simple issue of an overhead obstruction is examined.

An important factor in a no-clear-surface situation is the size and nature of the enclosure. Straightforward cavern-type formations can create a hazard, should silt or sand be stirred up. Finning action or contact can reduce visibility and thus obscure the path to open water. Should this happen, keep calm and immobile until the silt settles and sufficient visibility returns for an exit to be made. Such a situation is an indication that the penetration has been too great and that it really warranted the deployment of a guide line. It is much better to take precautions than to run this kind of risk. It is also important that any dives of this nature, which push limits, are well planned and supported. In particular, an adequate breathing-gas supply is

A no-clear-surface dive

essential and by this stage most recreational divers will have made the step up to a back-up independent breathing-gas supply such as a pony cylinder and regulator or a twin-cylinder configuration.

Swim-throughs are another form of no-clear-surface situation that prove very attractive to divers and may be formed by natural rock formations, accumulations of large boulders, or tangled, broken wreckage. Small or narrow passages such as these offer abrasion and collision hazards – this is often the moment where divers gain a real awareness of their underwater size and profile. Remember that light refraction through the mask lens makes underwater size and distance judgement quite difficult. Avoid dangling equipment as much as possible because besides offering snagging possibilities it can stir up silt and cause environmental damage. Do not attempt this kind of diving if either you or your buddy feel at all unsure or have any concerns regarding breathing-gas supply or if the visibility is limited.

Wreck diving is one of the most
popular types of diving

A wreck now home to a variety of marine life

Wreck diving

Surveys show that wreck diving is the favourite pastime of many recreational divers. In most locations wrecks are quickly colonised by a wide variety of marine life. The juxtaposition of these underwater life forms and man-made structures creates a uniquely fascinating panorama. The wreck itself creates an underwater 'atmosphere' which many find irresistible, triggering research into the history of the vessel and its initial loss. Many books have been written giving detailed information on either particular maritime disasters or cataloguing the wrecks of a certain period or geographical area. For the truly committed wreck addict there are numerous avenues of research.

Interest in wreck diving can be prompted by a variety of causes, from reports from other divers, seeing an article in a diving magazine, reading one of the many dive guide booklets produced on a certain area, a wreck symbol on a chart, talking to local fishermen about underwater 'snag' areas or reading a story about the loss of a ship.

Underwater wreckage

Using some form of shot-line or an anchor line, the wreck site can be reached with the minimum of time, effort and expenditure of valuable breathing gas. Then the fun begins! Obviously all wrecks are not the same, but just how different they can be can

Underwater wreckage

Initially, identifying parts of a ship can be difficult

be extremely bewildering. Firstly, there will be the differences between various types of ships, with even mass-produced series such as the famous American 'Liberty' ships showing quite marked individuality. However, it is the cause and location of the loss that can have the most profound effects on the form of the wreck. If the wreckage is relatively shallow, such as 30m or less in the North Atlantic, wave action will quickly cause the ship to break apart. The highly oxygenated water will accelerate this process by faster rusting of steel plates and structure. In really shallow, storm-exposed locations it can take just a few winters for much of a steel wreck to be reduced to a skeleton of beams and ribs, with non-ferrous fittings and heavier equipment such as engines, boilers, generators and winches scattered among them. Wooden vessels and parts can disappear equally rapidly, especially in warmer waters, with marine creatures such as the Teredo worm boring into and consuming the timber.

The cause of the loss will also have a bearing on the condition of the wreck. On ships sunk by mines, torpedoes, bombs or gunfire, the effects of this destruction will be apparent. So, too, will those ships that have sunk as a result of collision with another vessel, or obstruction such as a rock or reef. Structural failure or breaking apart in heavy weather will also be reflected in the subsequent appearance of the wreck. Even the collision with the sea bed can inflict further damage to the unfortunate ship.

This being the case, it is likely that as your early wreck dives will be on relatively shallow sites, you will encounter a puzzling heap of scrap metal and maybe even wonder what all the fuss was about. Persevere a little. Try to make some sense of muddled wreckage and you will discover a ship and something of its history. Look for easily identifiable objects such as an engine, a boiler, an anchor winch or a propeller shaft. These can give you an idea of the orientation of the ship, an idea of its size and your relative position among the wreckage. Quite possibly the cargo may provide some clues, although on shallow wrecks this may well have been salvaged or dispersed. The action of waves and currents may also have moved various parts of the wreck, with sand and silt possibly burying and hiding large sections. Most likely, your earlier wrecks will be well known and a description or drawing of what to expect will help in its exploration, but even so it is interesting to observe clues as to their identification. Clues to a ship's identity could be how many propellers there are or the location of certain structures – such as the bridge – or the type of engine or how much cargo space there is. While objects such as the ship's bell or wheel – which may have an engraved name and date – are the desired means of identification, many wrecks are identified by such things as a manufacturer's reference number on a piece of equipment, or a fragment of pottery from the galley bearing the shipping line crest. Make sure you avoid the worst symptoms of wreck fever and leave everything in place, observing both maritime law and the Divers' Code of Conduct. If you have to take anything from a wreck it should only be photographs and memories.

The ideal way of navigating your way around a wreck is to know what you are looking at. If you have a good idea of the appearance of the ship before it was wrecked, you can much more easily make sense of the jumbled mass of scrap scattered around the sea bed. A lot of information can be gained from photographs and drawings of the ship. For the total wreck enthusiast, equally valuable is the real-life study of as many ships as possible before you dive. While it is unlikely that you can tour a sister ship, visits to as many different types of ship as possible will give you a much better understanding of their construction and the appearance of their various structures and fittings. Visit the engine room, the bridge, look at the anchor winch, observe the general placement of fittings around the vessel. This kind of experience will enable you to orient yourself much more rapidly when wreck diving. However, be careful to be sensitive in the way you conduct your research. Sailors will naturally feel a little uncomfortable guiding you around their home if they think it is just to help you find your way round it should it sink!

A diver peers into the hatch of a shipwreck

Wreck exploration

Good preparation and planning will help minimise the risks when wreck diving, as will following sensible exploration procedures and attitudes. Most pleasurable wreck exploration is carried out in the open water around the wreck structure, entry being restricted to large spaces that are not too difficult to navigate or exit. Greatly reduced visibility, small, enclosed spaces and deep penetration inside wrecks have much in common with the highly specialised area of cave diving and require similar high levels of planning, preparation and experience.

The diving equipment on the market today places fairly drastic limitations on our underwater duration. This demands careful planning of all parts of the dive, but obviously the return to the surface is a particularly critical phase as that is when breathing-gas supplies will be reduced, yet decompression procedures need to be followed. It is essential, as the nature of the dive becomes more challenging, that a simple and certain return path is always available to the diver. Additionally, pre-planned decision points and criteria must be established and included in the dive plan. In wreck exploration where visibility or orientation may be difficult or where return to the shot or anchor line

Heavier equipment is the last thing to
disintergate on wrecks

Using a distance line on a wreck dive

is required, guide or bottom lines are used to ensure return routes and breathing-gas levels are used to provide a limit to how far a diver can explore away from the shot or anchor line.

The greater challenge of wreck diving and the hazards that may be encountered such as sharp structures, silt, sand, reduction in light levels and the presence of fishing nets or lines, increases substantially the importance of back-up equipment and procedures. In particular, breathing-gas supplies are crucial and most wreck divers regard a pony cylinder and totally separate second regulator as a minimum to provide an independent back-up breathing-gas supply. For deeper and therefore possibly darker wrecks, a larger back-up supply is needed so equipment configuration such as twin cylinders must be considered.

If visibility is reduced, orientation is difficult or divers must return to the shot or anchor line, the commonest form of guide line is a personal bottom line and reel – usually deployed and recovered by the lead diver. Many divers use a reel and line similar to that used for SMB/DSMB. The buddy diver simply follows along this line and, if visibility reduces further, holds the line to prevent diver separation. The line is usually around 1 to 2mm in diameter and made of white, braided

nylon to minimise kinking problems and maximise visibility. Many divers add some form of periodic distance marking to show the deployed length. Most personal reels can comfortably accommodate around 70m of such line and some can cope with more. Some consideration of the use of floating or non-floating line is also useful. Floating line can be easier to locate, but is an additional entrapment hazard for the divers, not only to the buddy pair using the line but others divers who may be diving on the wreck. Weighted line could be used but the reel and line will be heavier and as it is generally thicker than SMB/DSMB line so the size of reel required for a given length will be larger. Weighted line can be more difficult to locate if there is any silt, and can have an adverse effect on visibility by disturbing the silt.

Using a bottom or distance line needs thought and practise. The line, usually with a karabiner attachment, should be carefully attached to something secure near the shot or anchor line. Divers should ensure that it is not attached to something sharp in case it cuts the line. It can be attached to the shot-line, but care should be taken that it is securely fastened and will not ride up the shot-line. The distance line should then be paid out, maintaining tension to avoid it drifting upwards.

Wreck exploration

Deeper wrecks are less likely to disintegrate

A diver inspects an open wreck

The buddy pair should also take care not to catch their own fins in the line – finning side by side with the line being deployed between them is generally the best option should the buddy need to hold the line. The distance travelled away from the shot or anchor line may mean a considerable length of line being deployed and when exploring a wreck there will be an inevitable change of direction. To maintain the tension of the line and to avoid entanglement, the line can be temporarily secured to a piece of wreckage at a suitable or change of direction point. Winding or belaying the line around a piece of wreckage (with no sharp edges or causing damage to marine growth) keeps the line tensioned and near to the wreckage, but should also be easily detachable on the return journey.

While detailed depth and time gas-consumption calculations are an important part of wreck dive planning, certain overall strategic decisions also need to be made. If return to the shot/anchor line is necessary, the most commonly adopted strategy is the 'one third out, one third back, one third for ascent and reserve' rule, which is typically applied to the contents gauge reading. This means a diver starting the dive with a 200-bar reading would limit the outward journey and start the return at a gauge reading of 133

bar. This is a good broad-brush approach, but on long, deep dives that require extended decompression this may be too simplistic, so more refined and detailed calculation is essential. Of course, it is important that any such calculations are meaningful and, as one of the significant variables is breathing rate, every endeavour must be made to establish a practical range for your personal breathing rate, particularly in the expected conditions of the planned dive.

Most shipwrecks occur in or close to navigable waters, so the dangers posed by other surface vessels must be considered. As these waters are frequently tidal, the implications of short tidal windows and having to perform safety or decompression stops in moving water must be taken into account in dive planning and assessing the suitability of members of the diving party. If the dive plan does not necessitate a return to the shot/anchor line, divers should each carry a DSMB. Using an SMB on a wreck dive has inherent dangers of line catching on wreckage and is not advised. However, a DSMB is needed to mark the divers ascent point for the surface cover and may also be required for any decompression stops. Deploying a DSMB from a wreck for the ascent needs to be done avoiding any obstructions. The buddy pair needs to plan who is deploying the DSMB, the one that is not used is a backup for that diver in case of separation. It is also strongly recommended that even if return to the shot/anchor line is planned, divers should carry their own DSMBs. Should anything happen to prevent a normal return, the divers can ascend using a DSMB.

As havens for marine life, wrecks are often thought of as important fishing locations. This means many wrecks are festooned with snagged fishing equipment. The strength and near-invisibility of such lines and nets increase the chances of becoming entangled while wreck diving. Using a torch, divers can often pick up the glint of the near invisible, monofilament nets. By keeping aware of what is around you at all times and moving carefully, these nets can be avoided. With the risk of fishing line being present when wreck diving, a knife with a serrated net/rope blade or specifically designed serrated-blade net cutters should always be carried. Also, maximum use should be made of the buddy system to solve such situations. If a diver does get caught in line, the most important action is to stop and see if they can release themselves, but this should be done slowly and carefully to avoid further entanglement. If the diver needs help then the buddy can assist. It is worth remembering that lines cut more easily when under tension.

Techniques should also be mastered for finning and manoeuvring in silt-lined or rusty environments. One technique is to progress by gently moving the upper fin over a lower fin which is held so as to protect the bottom silt from disturbance. When using open-circuit scuba equipment, vertical movements are frequently initiated simply by adjusting the level of inhalation or exhalation. Finger 'walking' and careful use of strategic handholds is also practised, but care must be taken to avoid the razor-sharp edges that rusted steel can hide, and also the risk of damage both from and to various types of marine growth. Even the diver's exhaust bubbles can disturb silt or rust and adversely affect visibility. On early swim-through experiences it is often preferable for the more experienced diver to follow the less-experienced diver as then they are often better placed to cope with the reduced visibility and able to aid the less experienced diver in case of entanglement.

Wreck divers need to develop a three-dimensional sense of spatial awareness. Their normal body size is increased by their diving equipment and the size and shape of the volume they occupy changes with different activities. It should go without saying that perfect buoyancy control is essential. Complete non-disturbance of the wreck may not be feasible, but besides the possibility of becoming snagged, divers must be aware that any disturbance may also dislodge sections of wreckage. Incidents have occurred where the collapse of sections of wreck has been triggered, sometimes trapping exploring divers. Before entering or going under a section of wreckage, try to evaluate its structural integrity to ensure that further exploration is sensible. Most wreck-diving incidents have their roots in divers attempting levels of activity they are not yet ready for. The motto 'If in doubt, don't do it' may well be an appropriate one to follow!

As with most diving techniques, it is important to follow a learning curve of progressive difficulty, ensuring risks are not compounded by lack of suitable experience. Experience should be built up gradually as should the level of difficulty of the exploration. One of the most common features of wreck-based incidents is that of divers being exposed to challenging conditions that they are not yet properly qualified to cope with. Some open wrecks offer arches or wide tunnels of metal 'swim throughs' in places where a guide line is unnecessary as the exit can be clearly seen from the entrance, but care still needs to be taken not to disturb silt or sand. Many wrecks also have large, open holds or holes with what appears to be an easy entry/exit point. However, as light levels will fall and with the strong probability of silt, sand or rust disturbance inside, divers must take extreme care. Should anything go wrong inside – such as loss of gas supply or disturbance of silt so you lose your buddy or the exit point – the situation becomes dangerous. This type of wreck entry should be done slowly and carefully with the more experienced diver leading the entry phase and using a distance line secured outside the opening. This allows the divers to maintain contact with their exit point and, if necessary, return to it by a defined route. Such exploration needs to be agreed and planned by both divers, not everyone enjoys this extension of wreck diving. Planning and practise both of line deployment, positioning of divers relative to each other, ensuring both have torches and above all ensuring adequate gas supply and monitoring needs careful consideration. Initially, choose sites that are not prone to dangerous loss of visibility from disturbed silt, and where the entanglement risk is minimal. From this start you can slowly build your experience and enjoyment of wreck diving.

Ice diving

A safety rope is always used when ice diving

Ice diving

Okay, it is very difficult to justify why people ice dive other than giving a 'Because it is there' answer. But, given the opportunity, it is an experience you should not let pass. Watching your exhaust bubbles career around on the underside of the ice as they coalesce to form surreal shapes does have a certain fascination. So, too, does 'standing' upside down on the frozen surface, looking at an inverted world beyond your fins. Whatever your reason, with a little extra training and a lot of the right support, ice diving is an activity open to the majority of qualified divers.

Ice diving is an obvious example of no-clear-surface diving. However, the techniques used in no-clear-surface diving are merely a starting point, which need to be adapted for this very specific type of diving. In the first place, there is typically only one entry and exit point and it is essential that this can be easily located and reached at all times during the dive. Quite often a dive torch or strobe light is suspended underwater

by the hole to guide divers back. To prevent diver-to-surface separation a safety rope, usually 10mm braided nylon, is firmly attached to each diver by means of a body loop or harness worn underneath the BC. Some 30 to 50m in length, the other end of this line is attached to a secure spike or ice screw near the entry/exit point. This safety line is paid out and recovered by a tender who keeps the line free from entanglement and taut enough for the diver to be able to use it for signalling. Dive regulators will need to be environmentally protected to minimise the possibility of cold-induced free-flows. While a free-flowing regulator is difficult to cope with, as long as it can be retained in the mouth it can still be breathed from and the diver should immediately make his way back to the exit point. However, as ice diving is an extreme version of no-clear-surface diving, it is necessary to have a second, independent back-up gas supply should the worst happen.

Ice dives tend to take place at shallow depths

Ice diving

Ice diving requires good thermal protection

While diving under ice is certainly a cool activity, with good thermal protection such as a drysuit, thick undersuit, gloves and hood, underwater temperatures are usually comfortably sustainable for a 15 to 30-minute recreational dive. Further thermal protection for the difficult-to-protect face can be obtained by using a full-face mask, but that will demand further specialised training. Wet gloves provide some thermal protection for the hands, but this can be improved by using dry gloves that seal to the drysuit sleeves. Surprisingly, it is at the surface rather than underwater where sustaining body temperatures often tends to be a greater problem. With air temperatures cold enough to create the ice cover, even a light wind can create serious wind-chill difficulties, especially when wet after a dive. Wearing windproof clothing, particularly immediately after the dive, can help. Consider erecting a tent or other shelter close to the site to protect divers while they kit up prior to the dive and de-kit and change into warm clothing afterwards. A shelter also

offers diving equipment protection from the elements – a carelessly placed regulator may well freeze to the ice! All steps should be taken to avoid the likelihood of any of the party suffering from hypothermia and all of the diving party should keep an eye out for possible symptoms. The surface party will need similar protection and should be clad in warm windproof and waterproof clothing. Pay attention to footwear, many dive tenders prefer to wear crampons for better grip, besides being themselves attached to a secure point.

It is essential that when any ice diving is taking place that an experienced, fully equipped safety diver is ready to dive should any diver fail to respond to signals or should another underwater situation require it. The safety diver will also need a tender and should have a longer safety line than any of the other divers, typically by a factor of 50 per cent. Limit the number of divers in the water at any one time in order to simplify dive management and minimise line-tangling risk. Different coloured ropes are often

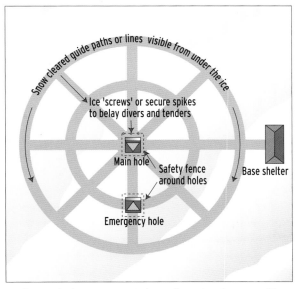

Ice diving requires considerable site preparation and surface support. Ensure the ice can support the equipment and personnel lo Chain saws are often used to cut holes which must then be marked to protect others. Sleds are often useful to transport equipmen across the ice. Fixed guide lines may also be attached to the underside of the ice.

used to help identify the different divers. Both tender and diver should be competent in communicating using a basic set of rope signals and should agree the dive plan in advance. There should be an advance contingency plan for all foreseeable events that might demand safety-diver intervention, but typically the first action would be to follow the safety line of the diver with the problem. If for some reason a diver has become separated from the line, the safety diver swims slightly anti-clockwise of the last known direction of the missing diver to their full line extent and then makes a clockwise sweeping search.

Mostly, ice diving takes place in frozen-over ponds or lakes and it is useful to have some idea of likely underwater conditions before making the dive, usually from a prior dive there in warmer conditions. Generally speaking, underwater visibility is good but light levels are usually reduced, especially if the ice is thick or there is snow cover over the ice, so torches may be necessary. First, make sure the ice is strong enough to support any surface activity. If there is any doubt, surface operations must be shore-based. Given a good, solid ice cover, a suitable hole needs to be cut to provide access for the divers. Ideally this will be triangular with 2 to 3m sides. Holes are drilled at

the three points and the ice in between is cut out. The triangular shape provides maximum support for the divers during their entry and exit.

Snow-covered ice can have paths cleared so exposing the ice and creating a pattern to aid the divers in locating the exit. The pattern generally adopted will have straight paths radiating out from the hole plus one or two circular 'range' paths, the furthest being laid out at the limit of the diver's safety line. This creates a pattern somewhat like a dartboard in the snow.

With such low temperatures, most underwater life-forms will tend to be rather sluggish as they try to conserve energy. Respect this state of affairs and avoid disturbing them. On most ice dives there is no real reason to dive deep, as the most interesting point of the dive will be the ice itself. This means that it is likely to be the cold rather than decompression that limits dive times, but as much ice diving is performed in high-altitude lakes, lower-than-usual ambient pressure conditions may apply and should be taken into consideration when dive planning.

Cave diving

Caves can provide stunning underwater vistas

Cave diving

Strictly speaking, this section has no place in this book. Cave diving is not the province of the recreational diver and really belongs to recreational cavers, who need to dive because their cave is full of water. If, as a recreational diver, you want to explore flooded caves, you are strongly advised to find a reputable caving organisation and learn to cave. At some stage in the development of your caving expertise your diving knowledge and experience will become useful, but to explore caves, wet or dry, you need a competency in caving that this book cannot provide. That said, there are some interesting points that we as divers can take from our caving colleagues and these points may also help you in deciding whether cave diving is of suffi-

cient interest for you to take it up seriously.

Cave diving certainly has some parallels with both wreck penetration and ice diving. While often sharing the single entry/exit point pattern, a major difference is that the no-clear-surface conditions tend to extend for much greater distances when exploring a cave system. While there are cave systems with short water-filled sumps to be negotiated, such caves are going to involve much more caving than diving and so tend to attract cavers rather than divers. On the other hand there are underground systems with very long, submerged passages where diving skills are a necessary addition to those of caving. To achieve the desired penetration in such systems, the cave diver

Head-mounted lamps are often used by cave divers

Cave diving requires proper training and equipment

often needs to carry large amounts of breathing gas, so much so that sometimes cylinders have to be relayed in and positioned at various staging points to enable exploration to advance. Whatever the amount of breathing gas required, one golden rule applies – one third for inward travel, one third for return travel and one third for emergencies. A high degree of competency in the handling of equipment is called for, often in cramped and difficult conditions.

While it can be dark inside wrecks and even under ice, darkness is a constant in caving and adequate underwater lighting is a major preoccupation for the cave diver. Caving organisations rightly regard waterproof lamps as the weakest link in their diving equipment, believing lamp failure is a matter of when, not if. As a result, cave divers carry three light sources, a main torch and two good reliable backups. A distance line is another feature that cave diving has in common with wreck diving, but as the distances concerned are so much greater the reels have to be bigger and cavers prefer as strong a line as possible. Depth, too, can be a major obstacle for cave divers, with both narcosis and oxygen toxicity posing barriers that can only be overcome by moving to Trimix or other exotic solutions. Because cave diving involves

being long distances from the start base, many cave divers ensure a high degree of equipment redundancy. Carrying two independent breathing-gas systems is common – often side rather than back-mounted, as this can provide a better profile in some tight passages.

While there are similarities between cave and normal scuba diving, there are many differences. The training in both caving and cave diving is essential, so do not be tempted to just venture in to 'see the beginning' – silt is the norm in many caves and without proper equipment the beginning could turn out to be the end.

New challenges await you

And then...

You started this journey to discover more about dive leading. Hopefully, you are now persuaded that it is a journey worth taking and are possibly well down the path to gaining a higher certification. If so, you can be proud of yourself. You are now among the top 50 per cent of the diving community and have reached a stage where you are putting something back into the development of our passion. With each new experience you gain, you find new challenges revealed; with each question you answer, you find even more intriguing ones to pose. To know that this process is never ending is strangely satisfying – the excitement of new discoveries will be never ending. As a dive leader you reach the first officially recognised level for employment in the recreational dive industry. Whether you choose to lead and guide others on their underwater adventures voluntarily or as a means of earning a living is irrelevant. The process is the same, the experience is the same, and the pleasure you provide to others is the same.

Of course, there is still more to learn, still more experience to be gained. This book has introduced many topics which are worthy of a book on their own. Most serious diver-training agencies offer a wealth of skill development courses that will enable you to develop specialist knowledge and expertise. Pursuing your interests with friends, in a club, a school or a resort, diving offers you a lifetime of new experiences.

Just like the diving itself, the satisfaction from leading others underwater can become addictive. How can you satisfy this craving? There is only one way – you will have to dive more and gain more experience and more knowledge. Expand and adapt your diving techniques and you have the key to a lifetime of exploration. ■

Where will your diving take you?

Appendix one – First aid

The recovery position

The recovery position for an unstable environment such as a boat, note that one arm is arranged behind the body

First aid

The aim of administering first aid in any diving incident must be to preserve the life of the casualty – and all involved – with the minimum of intervention, in order to limit the effects of the incident and to promote recovery. Avoid compounding the situation by taking foolhardy risks to recover the casualty. With water-centred incidents, the correct actions in order of priority are:

- Reach for the casualty.
- Throw flotation aids.
- Wade out to the casualty or use surface transport or flotation to reach the casualty.
- Swim to the casualty. However, swimming alone should be considered a poorer, final option.

The sequence of action can be summarised as 'assessment, diagnosis and treatment'. Action priorities in order of importance are 'airway, breathing and circulation' (ABC), followed by incidents involving major bleeding and other conditions. Should there be more than one casualty, you should prioritise by treating the non-breathing casualty first, followed by the breathing but unconscious casualty and then any casualties suffering from major bleeding.

Drowning

In order to ensure a viable airway, the casualty's mouth and nose must be clear of the water, hence the need for divers to know how to lift non-breathing casualties to the surface. Ideally this should be followed by immediate removal of the casualty from the water. If this is not possible, stabilise the casualty at the surface and if he or she is still not breathing, commence artificial ventilation (AV). In-water AV can be administered either by mouth-to-nose or mouth-to-mouth resuscitation, with mouth-to-nose generally preferred. The ability of a single rescuer is fairly limited, so efforts should be made to summon assistance and to move to a situation where exit from the water is possible. A balance has to be struck between maintaining an effective rate of AV and moving the casualty towards a water exit.

AV on its own will not be enough if circulation has stopped. In these circumstances cardiac compression (CC) will be needed, requiring that the casualty is supported on a firm surface such as a boat or on land. To give effective cardio-pulmonary resuscitation (CPR) you should obtain appropriate training – courses are offered by most diver-training agencies.

Barotrauma/DCI

The most serious pressure-related injuries (known as barotrauma) result from incorrect dive profiles as well as rapid ascents resulting in either decompression illness (DCI) or a burst lung or lungs. First-aid actions are the same for both.

Symptoms are
- Weakness, paralysis, numbness, tingling
- Vision problems, balance problems, confusion, convulsions, unconciousness
- Large-joint pain
- Skin itchiness or rash

Treatment
- Arrange immediate evacuation to recompression facilities
- Lay casualty flat, administer 100-per-cent oxygen
- If no other injuries or nausea, give isotonic fluids or water
- DO NOT attempt in-water treatment

Shock

In most accidents casualties will be suffering shock.

Symptoms are
- Weakness, faintness, giddiness, anxiousness, restlessness
- Nausea, vomiting, thirst, cold clammy skin, profuse sweating
- Shallow rapid breathing, rapid weak pulse

Treatment
- Treat prime cause, keep quiet, reassure, keep warm and comfortable
- Lay down with legs raised (not if DCI involved), administer 100-per-cent oxygen
- Monitor condition, evacuate to medical attention

External bleeding

Look for signs of visible blood loss.

Treatment
- Direct pressure or indirect pressure to pressure points

Internal bleeding

Symptoms are
- Signs of shock without obvious blood loss
- Pain out of all proportion to visible damage
- Pattern bruising, coughing/spitting blood, blood in urine/faeces

Treatment:
- Treat as for shock
- Urgent evacuation
- Check and record breathing and pulse and level of response every ten minutes
- Put in recovery position if unconscious

Fractures

Symptoms are:
- Sound at initial break, visible bone ends/deformity/loss of power
- Pain, tenderness, swelling/bruising
- Shock

Treatment
- Keep immobilised where the casualty is lying
- Keep steady until splinted/gentle traction
- Support in the most comfortable position
- Dress open fractures before splinting
- Don't miss other less obvious conditions
- Treat for shock

Burns

Symptoms are:
- Severe pain at the site of injury, numbness if a deep burn
- Sometimes blistering, grey, charred, peeling skin
- Shock

Treatment
- Reassure casualty and cool affected area
- Remove constrictions and protect affected area
- DO NOT break blisters or apply lotions or adhesive dressings
- Treat for shock

Dislocations

Symptoms are
- Pain, limited or no articulation of joint
- Deformity or abnormal appearance, swelling and bruising

Treatment
- Support and keep limb steady in most comfortable position.
- DO NOT attempt to reset □

Appendix two – Buddy rescue

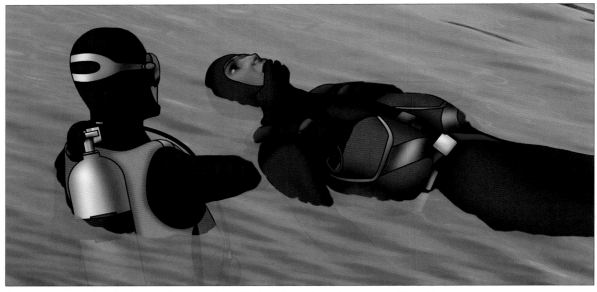

The forearm lever grip: grip the casualty's lower jaw while levering against his or her shoulder with your forearm as you commence artificial ventilation

A number of techniques are taught for buddy rescue from depth, but the prime considerations should be central to all. The overriding factor must be a return of the casualty to the surface in a speedy but controlled manner, followed by a prompt removal to appropriate expert care. During this process all efforts must be made to ensure contact with the casualty is maintained, that the casualty reaches and remains at the surface and that if needed artificial ventilation and cardiac compression are commenced as soon as possible. There should be no delay in seeking outside emergency aid.

Study of diving incident reports shows a number of attempted rescues fail because contact with the casualty is lost and the casualty subsequently does not arrive at the surface. This strongly suggests that the casualty should be made positively buoyant at an early stage of the rescue. Historically, strong emphasis has been placed on the removal of weight belts but again incident analysis shows this rarely occurs in real rescue situations. There are also the arguments that often the change in buoyancy this provides may be insignificant, or if it is significant once removed

subsequent buoyancy control may be impossible.

A controlled ascent may can be achieved using the buoyant rescue technique illustrated. Depending on the equipment configuration of the casualty different methods of ensuring buoyancy are used. The key is to simplify as much as possible the buoyancy control problems that will face the rescuer. If the two divers have only BCs to provide controllable air spaces, the situation is straightforward. The simplest solution is for casualty's BC to be used to provide a small, controllable positive buoyancy to assist the ascent. Should separation occur there is then a much greater chance that the casualty will at least reach the surface.

If the casualty is wearing a drysuit then that will almost certainly be a buoyancy source that must be taken into consideration. If fitted with an automatic dump valve on the upper body it may well be possible to achieve a controlled buoyant ascent as above, using the casualty's BC. In some circumstances it may be more appropriate to use the casualty's drysuit to provide ascent buoyancy if that provides the simplest solution to controlling the suit's buoyancy. Once at the surface the casualty's BC will normally provide the best and most reliable buoyant support. In all cases the rescuer must also take account of changing buoyancy during the ascent from their own BC or drysuit.

A great deal is talked about how to grip the casualty, with attention paid to BC and drysuit controls. The two essentials must be retaining a grip on the casualty and achieving as much control over the ascent speed as possible. A face-to-face position with the rescuer slightly below the casualty will usually meet these needs. One hand can then be used to make a secure grip, normally using the drysuit inflator or some part of the casualty's BC, the other hand being free to operate any buoyancy controls.

Should it be impossible to provide buoyancy to the candidate at depth, an alternative technique is for the rescuer to face the casualty and use a leg-scissor grip around the casualty's upper body and then use their own buoyancy system to achieve the ascent. This technique may not be feasible with some equipment configurations such as twin-sets. If all else fails a swimming ascent will be needed and it is very likely that weight-belt removal will have a beneficial effect. A number of authorities advocate that in swimming lifts the top and bottom of casualty's dive cylinder are gripped as this helps keep the rescuer's legs free for finning and also helps the rescuer maintain direct vertical progress. Remember in all emergency ascents, extra care should be payed to proper exhalation and never hold your breath.

Once at the surface – with the casualty's buoyancy stabilised and distress signalled – artificial ventilation (AV) must be commenced as rapidly as possible on any non-breathing casualty. This can usually be most effective using a mouth-to-nose technique. If the AV is to be successful, it is essential that there is a clear airway, so a good neck extension must be achieved. A practical way of ensuring this in the water is to use a grip on the lower jaw and lever against the casualty's shoulder with your forearm as you ventilate. Once an AV rhythm has been established – if help is not going to arrive – it may be necessary for the rescuer to try and make progress to safety such as a shore or immobile boat. If such a tow is necessary the rescuer must still make all efforts to maintain an effective rate of AV, which must continue throughout any de-kitting and the removal of the casualty from the water. An unconscious non-breathing casualty can only receive the required attention out of the water. AV is only a means of buying time to get them there. If help, in the form of a boat, can get to the rescuer then the balance is in favour of administering AV until it arrives. If a tow is required, then AV must of necessity be compromised as the balance swings to the urgent removal of the casualty.

Top, using a leg grip to bring a casualty to the surface; bottom, using a BC lift to bring a casualty to the surface

Most diver-straining agencies require that dive leaders undergo specialist training in courses in both first aid and rescue. For more information on specific training courses and support materials contact BSAC headquarters on 0151 350 6200 or see the website www.bsac.org.

Appendix three – Wind and sea classification

Beaufort description	Beaufort force	Sea condition	Land condition	Wind speed knots
Calm	0	Flat and mirror-like.	Calm, smoke rises vertically.	0
Light air	1	Small, smooth ripples.	Smoke drift shows wind direction.	1–3
Light breeze	2	Non-breaking wavelets.	Leaves rustle, wind can be felt on skin, weather vanes operate.	4–6
Gentle breeze	3	Large wavelets with occasional white caps.	Leaves and twigs move, light flag extended.	7–10
Moderate breeze	4	Small waves with frequent white caps.	Dust and paper raised, small branches moving.	11–16
Fresh breeze	5	Moderate waves with many white caps.	Small leafy trees sway.	17–21
Strong breeze	6	Large waves forming, foaming crests, possibly spray.	Large branches move, wind whistles in overhead wires and rigging, umbrellas difficult to handle.	22–27
Near gale	7	Heaped-up seas with foam streaks.	Whole trees in motion and difficulty experienced in walking against the wind.	28–33
Gale	8	Moderately high waves with crests often carried as spindrift.	Movement definitely impeded, twigs broken from trees.	34–40
Strong gale	9	High waves with breaking crests, foam carried by wind may affect visibility.	Slight structural damage to slates and chimneys.	41–47
Storm	10	Very high waves with long overhanging crests, much foam giving the sea a white appearance. Visibility affected.	Not frequently experienced inland, trees uprooted and considerable structural damage produced.	48–55
Violent storm	11	Exceptionally high waves which may temporarily obscure small and medium boats from view. Wave crests blown to produce large areas of froth and visibility obscured.	Rarely experienced inland, widespread structural damage.	56–63
Hurricane	12	Air filled with foam and spray, sea completely white with driven spray. Visibility seriously obscured.	Confined to coastal zones with devastating effects.	64+

Sea state	Average wave height metres/feet	Average wind speed kph/knots	Description
0	0 / 0	0.9/0.5	Glassy
1	0.04/0.12	6.5/3.5	Rippled
2	0.31/1.0	21/11.5	Wavelets
3	0.72/2.4	35/19	Slight
4	1.63/5.4	45/25	Moderate
5	2.88/9.5	56/30	Rough
6	4.58/15	61/33	Very rough
7	6.71/22	69/37	High
8	11.7/39	89/48	Very high
9	19.9/66	118/64	Phenomenal

Appendix four– Qualifications

BSAC diver qualifications

BSAC First Class Diver

This grade demands a higher than average level of theoretical knowledge and organisational and personal diving skills. First Class Divers have a broad range of practical experience and are capable of planning, organising and leading advanced level diving expeditions. This grade is awarded following a nationally conducted assessment.

First Class Diver

BSAC Advanced Divers

This grade requires that divers have considerable diving experience and have developed their skills to a level that enables them to competently organise and lead diving expeditions. They will have additional experience in managing diving in a wide range of conditions and circumstances.

Advanced Diver

BSAC Dive Leaders

To reach this level divers will require considerable dive management and rescue management skills and be competent in organising and leading diving groups. Their dive planning, conduct and navigational abilities will qualify them to act as dive guides. This grade meets and exceeds the proposed European Level 3 diver standard.

BSAC Sports Divers

At this level, divers may dive autonomously to a depth of 35m in waters that match their previous training and experience. They can also conduct dives requiring in-water decompression and are trained in more comprehensive rescue skills, including basic surface resuscitation.

Dive Leader

Sports Diver

BSAC Ocean Divers

This grade allows divers to dive autonomously with others of the same or higher grades. Divers are trained to elementary buddy rescue level. Dives are limited to a depth of 20m operating in waters similar to those they have trained in. Ocean Divers are not trained to conduct dives requiring in-water decompression stops or to dive without more experienced surface support. This grade meets and exceeds the proposed European Level 2 diver standard.

Ocean Diver

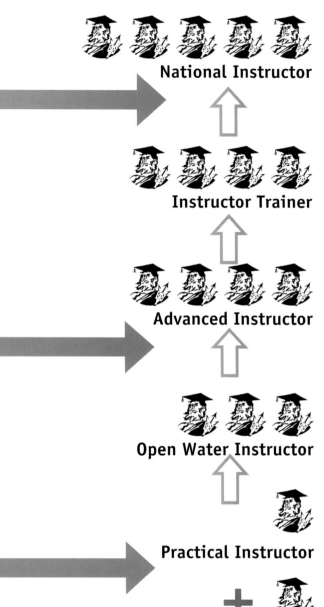

National Instructor

Instructor Trainer

Advanced Instructor

Open Water Instructor

Practical Instructor

+

Theory Instructor

BSAC instructor qualifications

BSAC National Instructor

To gain this qualification, the highest BSAC instructor grade, the candidate must have previously qualified as a BSAC First Class Diver. National Instructors are used in the training and assessment of other instructors and as team leaders in the BSAC Instructor Training Scheme.

BSAC Instructor Trainer

A BSAC Advanced Instructor who has received further instruction and assessment enabling him or her to participate in the BSAC Instructor Training Scheme as a trainer of other instructors.

BSAC Advanced Instructor

A BSAC Open Water Instructor with considerable diving and instructional experience who has received further training and assessment. Advanced Instructors are qualified to teach a wide range of skills and to supervise the work of other instructors.

BSAC Open Water Instructor

A BSAC instructor who is qualified to teach both theoretical and practical diving in classrooms, and in both sheltered and open-water environments.

BSAC Practical Instructor

A BSAC instructor who has received training in practical instructional techniques and limited assessment which allows him or her to provide instruction in practical diving skills.

BSAC Theory Instructor

A BSAC instructor who has received training in instructional techniques and theory assessment which allows him or her to provide instruction in diving theory subjects. ☐

Note: All BSAC instructors are trained and assessed through the nationally organised BSAC Instructor Training Scheme.

Minimum diver level required in order to take instructor qualification

Appendix five – Conversions and calculations

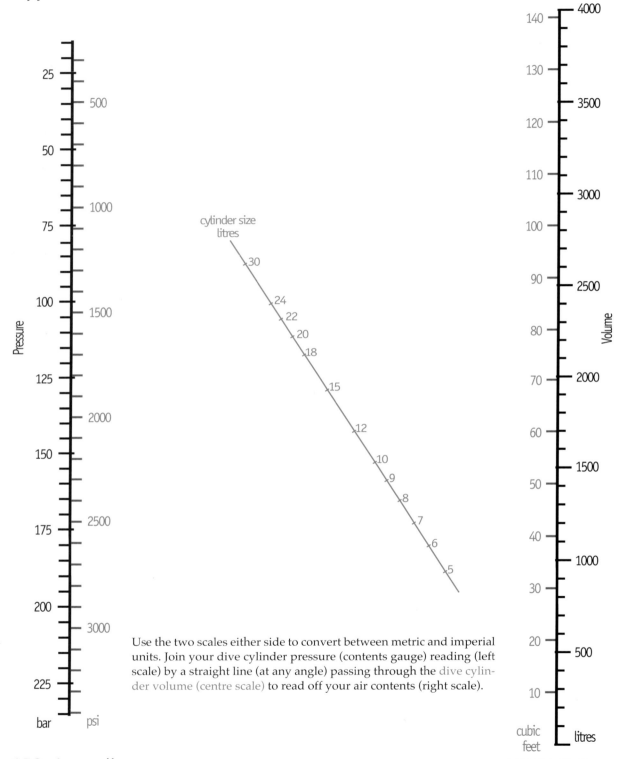

Pressure

bar	psi
25	500
50	1000
75	1500
100	2000
125	
150	2500
175	3000
200	
225	

cylinder size
litres

30
24
22
20
18
15
12
10
9
8
7
6
5

Volume

140 — 4000
130 — 3500
120
110 — 3000
100
90 — 2500
80 — 2000
70
60 — 1500
50
40 — 1000
30 — 500
20
10

cubic feet   litres

Use the two scales either side to convert between metric and imperial units. Join your dive cylinder pressure (contents gauge) reading (left scale) by a straight line (at any angle) passing through the dive cylinder volume (centre scale) to read off your air contents (right scale).

Conversions and calculations

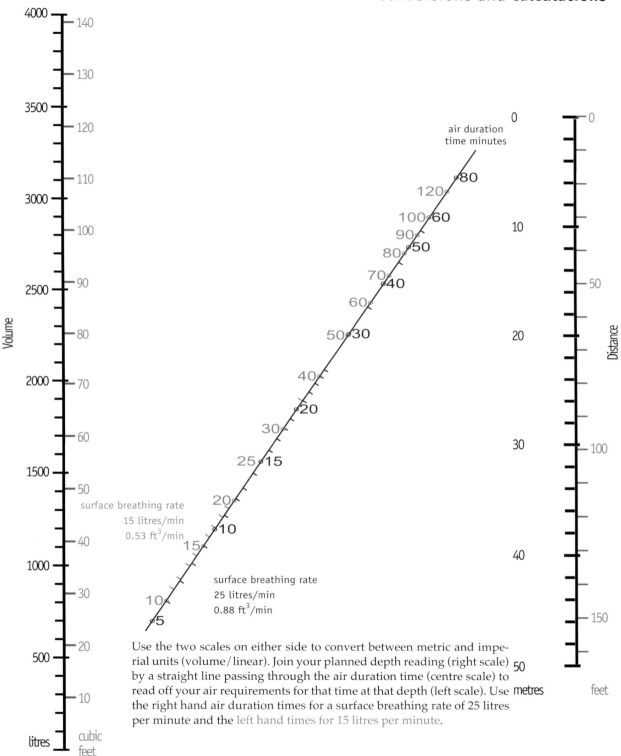

Volume

4000
140
130
3500
120
3000
110
100
2500
90
2000
80
70
1500
60
50
1000
40
500
30
20
10

litres

cubic feet

air duration time minutes

0

120
100
90
80
70
60
50
40
30
25 15
20
15
10
5

surface breathing rate
15 litres/min
0.53 ft³/min

surface breathing rate
25 litres/min
0.88 ft³/min

0
80
60
50
40
30
20
10

Distance

0
10
50
20
30
100
40
150
50

metres   feet

Use the two scales on either side to convert between metric and imperial units (volume / linear). Join your planned depth reading (right scale) by a straight line passing through the air duration time (centre scale) to read off your air requirements for that time at that depth (left scale). Use the right hand air duration times for a surface breathing rate of 25 litres per minute and the left hand times for 15 litres per minute.

Appendix six – Code of Conduct

Divers' Code of Conduct

The BSAC Divers' Code of Conduct is designed to encourage good behaviour at dive sites and when diving, and to ensure that divers do not come into conflict with other water users.

Dive planning

Contact the nearest BSAC branch or dive school local to the dive site for advice on local conditions and regulations.

At the dive site

- Obtain permission before diving in restricted areas, such as harbours, estuaries or private waters.
- Thank all the relevant parties before you leave and ensure any dues are paid.
- Avoid overcrowding sites and show consideration to other users.
- Park sensibly, avoiding obstruction and damage to verges. Use proper car parks and pay parking fees.
- Keep launching ramps and slipways clear and be economical with use of space.
- Keep the peace, do not operate compressors or boat and car engines unsociably.
- Do not litter. Close gates. Be careful about fires. Avoid any damage to land or crops.
- Obey special instructions such as National Trust rules, local bylaws and regulations about camping and caravanning.
- Remember, our equipment makes divers conspicuous and bad behaviour can result in future restrictions.

In and on the water

- Make your boats identifiable, this can help rescue agencies and shows you have nothing to hide.
- Seek advice about, and permission for, launching and follow it.
- Inform the coastguard or a responsible person of your operational plan and report when your diving is complete.
- Avoid diving near buoys, pots and pot markers.
- Ask local fishermen where it is advisable *not* to dive.
- Avoid disturbing local wildlife such as sea bird or seal colonies.

- Avoid diving in fairways or areas of heavy surface traffic and observe the International Regulations for Preventing Collisions at Sea. Commercial traffic usually has restricted manoeuvring capability.
- Always fly the diving flag when conducting diving operations, but not when the boat is in transit. Do not leave boats unattended.
- Do not come in to bathing beaches under power, do use any special approach lanes and avoid creating unnecessary wash in restricted waterways or moorings.
- Use surface marker buoys where appropriate.
- Respect local bylaws, regulations and customs.

On conservation

- Do not use a spear-gun when scuba diving.
- Collecting marine creatures of any kind is damaging to the environment and often subject to legal control. Take photographs and notes, not specimens.

On wrecks

- Do not dive on a designated, protected wreck site without specific authority. These are generally indicated on charts and marked by buoys or warning notices on the shore nearby.
- Do not disturb anything that appears to be of historical importance.
- If you discover a wreck, do not disturb anything and report its position and any other details to the relevant authorities.
- Be aware that many wrecks involved loss of life and as such can be sensitive areas and deserve respect.
- Follow the BSAC wreck policy – look, don't touch: more detailed advice on wreck diving is published on the BSAC website: www.bsac.org

Diving freedoms stem from responsible diving, it is up to us as divers to behave sensibly and sociably – and keep to the Divers' Code. ☐

Index

Index

Index

Photographs

Charles Hood:

Cover photograph by Charles Hood and post production by Julian Calverley. All other photographs by Charles Hood with the exception of those listed below.

Graeme Bruce:

page 65

Julian Calverley:

chapter breaks, pages 38; 48; 68; 116; 156.
website: www.calverley.co.uk

Deric Ellerby:

page 136

Andrew Hancock:

page 21 (left)

Guy Middleton:

page 46

National Hydrographic Office:

pages 23 (left); 40

Alex Misiewicz:

page 142

Gavin Newman:

pages 66; 140; 141

Simon Rogerson:

page 89

Rich Stevenson:

page 109 (left)

Lawson Wood:

chapter break, page 18

The British Sub-Aqua Club gratefully acknowledges the assistance provided by numerous members, schools, and friends in the diving trade in the development of this book.